THE ACTS OF THE APOSTLES

THE ACTS OF THE APOSTLES

TRANSLATED *from the* CODEX BEZÆ *with an* INTRODUCTION *on its* LUCAN ORIGIN *and importance by*

CANON J. M. WILSON, D.D.

WIPF & STOCK · Eugene, Oregon

Wipf and Stock Publishers
199 W 8th Ave, Suite 3
Eugene, OR 97401

The Acts of the Apostles
Translated from the Codex Bezae with an Introduction on its
Lucan Origin and Importance
By Wilson, J. M.
ISBN 13: 978-1-61097-123-2
Publication date 01/05/2011
Previously published by SPCK, 1923

PREFACE

IT is necessary to state quite explicitly that this little work is not intended or thought of as a contribution to scholarship or criticism, or as bearing on the great problem of the origin and reconstruction of the Western Text. The whole subject, besides being far beyond my powers, is not yet ripe for settlement. Work on it by eminent scholars has been going on for years, and is proceeding apace in England, Germany and the U.S.A. New materials are being discovered. It will receive the devoted attention of scholars for years to come.

Scholars and textual critics have ample material put before them. My sole aim is to give English readers of the New Testament some outline of the unusual interest connected with this problem of New Testament criticism; to indicate its importance and bearing on wide issues; and to place before them for the first time, in the case of one book, materials for judging for themselves one of the chief arguments used for what appears the most probable solution. In a word my aim is to promote Christian knowledge. To critics I would say:

In every work regard the writer's end,
Since none can compass more than they intend.

I acknowledge most gratefully the permission granted me by the Delegates and Syndics of the University Presses to make use of the Revised Version in the translation of the Acts of the Apostles given in this book.

JAMES M. WILSON.

COLLEGE, WORCESTER.
July 1923.

CONTENTS

	PAGE
I. INTRODUCTION	1

SECTION
1. The object of this Translation 1
2. Statement of the question that it raises . . . 1
3. The great importance of this text 2
4. Its decisive importance recognised by leading critics 2
5. Readers of English only are qualified to form a judgment from the translation alone 4
6. Outline of supplementary matters touched on in this Introduction 5
7. The internal evidence examined. Illustrations of omissions for the sake of brevity 5
8. Interest on various grounds of some of the omitted passages 6
9. Instances of some sentences rewritten . . . 7
10. Excisions few where St Luke appears to be quoting from documents supplied him 7
11. Excisions in the account of St Paul's first missionary journey, and probable inference 8
12. Importance of the fact supplied by this text in Acts xi. 28 9
13. St Luke's presence at Antioch throws light on one of the sources of his Gospel 11
14. Light is also thrown on St Luke's use of Q and on the history of Manaen 12
15. A further inference from St John's Gospel as to the history of Manaen 13
16. Importance of the Bezan text of the decree of the Council of Jerusalem in Acts xv. 14
17. The difference of the two texts 15
18. The nature of the arguments in support of either text of the decree 16

SECTION		PAGE
19.	Difficulties in accepting the ordinary text	16
20.	Difficulties removed by accepting the text in this codex as the true report of the decree	17
21.	The words "things strangled" a later interpolation unknown to the earliest texts	18
22.	The evidences, internal and external, for the view here advocated cumulative and convincing	19
23.	Confirmed by minor verbal alterations, and an avoidance in the revision of over-statement	20
24.	Confirmed further by the additions made by St Luke in the revision	21
25.	Some supplementary information	22
26.	A brief description of the Codex Bezæ	23
27.	The origin of the hypothesis that there were two Lucan originals of the MSS. of the Acts of the Apostles	25
28.	Why the ordinary text is preserved in so many MSS. and this text became so rare	26
29.	Were there also two original Lucan texts of his Gospel?	27
30.	Why this view of the value of the text in Codex Bezæ was not adopted by the Revisers in 1880	28
31.	Professor Hort's study of the texts of the New Testament of great value	29
32.	Scrivener's final remarks on the Greek text of the Codex Bezæ	30
33.	Why recent opinions of scholars are not here summarised	32
34.	Grounds on which late dates have often been assigned by critics to the writings usually regarded as Lucan	32
35.	Brief statement of results which follow from acceptance of the views above advocated	34

II. NOTE ON THE TRANSLATION . . 38

III. THE ACTS OF THE APOSTLES TRANSLATED FROM THE CODEX BEZÆ. . 39

I

INTRODUCTION

1. *The Object of this Translation*

A GLANCE at the translation that follows will shew the difference between this text and those from which our ordinary English versions are taken. The words in thick type are in the Codex Bezæ, briefly referred to as D, but not in our ordinary text; and the words in square brackets are in our ordinary text, but not in D. The object of this arrangement is to enable readers of the English New Testament to form a judgment on one of the most interesting and important problems of New Testament criticism lately brought before scholars, the Lucan origin of this remarkable text of the Acts. The lack of Greek scholarship, and that of other technical knowledge, do not disqualify anyone from forming an intelligent and independent opinion on one solution offered of the main question at issue.

2. *Statement of the question that it raises*

The main question is this. There must be some reason for the striking difference between this text and that with which we are familiar. It has come to be believed by some scholars that there is conclusive evidence, both external and internal, that St Luke wrote a first draft of the Acts, and then revised, rewrote, and somewhat shortened it in the copy which he sent to Theophilus at Antioch; and that each of these texts was preserved and naturally copied, again and again, for the use of Churches; and that thus there came to exist from the earliest period two texts of the Acts, a longer and a shorter, a Western—so called from its chief circulation in the West—and an Antiochian.

The oldest MSS. of the Acts that happen to survive (none are older, however, than the fourth century), and the great majority of the later MSS., are all Antiochian; and it is from these that both our Authorised and Revised Versions were translated. But it has chanced that a few MSS. survive which were derived from St Luke's first and longer draft; and of these the Codex Bezæ, known as D, now at Cambridge, is the oldest. These few and exceptional MSS. have been generally regarded, very naturally, but mistakenly, as full of strange later interpolations, and have therefore been disregarded as textual authorities. The belief that I speak of now is that the longer text, here for the first time shewn in English, is derived from St Luke's original and longer draft; and that the shorter text of our ordinary versions was formed from it by St Luke's own excision of what could be spared.

If this belief is well founded we have here additions and a correction to the Received Text of the New Testament; and, as it happens, additions and a correction of singular interest and importance.

3. *The great importance of this text*

I will state at once why these additions and this correction, though small in extent, are of such general interest and importance. It is not only because they clear up some long-standing obscurities, but that they are decisive as to the early date of the writing of the Acts, and consequently of the early dates of the Gospels. How important it is to be assured of these early dates needs no enforcement. It is obvious that early Christian writings, derived from personal knowledge or from contemporary testimony, are of a wholly different value, as evidence for the truth of the historic basis of our Christian faith, from writings of a hundred, or seventy, or even forty years later.

4. *Its decisive importance recognised by leading critics*

I have said that the additional matter and an omission in this text of the Acts are decisive as to the early date of its composition, if this text is accepted as really Lucan in origin. My own judgment on this question could carry no

INTRODUCTION 3

weight. But I will quote on this point two of the admittedly highest authorities on New Testament criticism, both of them reluctant witnesses, Harnack and Schmiedel.

Harnack in 1911 (*Date of the Acts...*, p. 93) writes: "I have now come to believe that there is a high probability in favour of an early date for the Lukan writings." He goes on to assign to the composition of them a date before the destruction of Jerusalem. He had previously written (*Acts of the Apostles*, Crown Edn. p. 250) that he had agreed with almost everyone in accepting the Eastern form of the decree in Acts xv. as the original. "Since that time, and, I may say, with great reluctance, and after long consideration, I have arrived at a different conclusion. I am not fond of correcting myself; but *magis amica veritas*." It was chiefly the external evidence that convinced Harnack.

And Dr P. S. Schmiedel, in his article on the Acts in the *Encyclopædia Biblica*, after urging every possible argument for a late date, states his conclusion as follows: "The date of Acts must accordingly be set down as somewhere between 105 and 130; or if the Gospel of Luke presupposes acquaintance with all the writings of Josephus, between 110 and 130." But then follows this remarkable sentence: "*The conclusions reached in the foregoing sections would have to be withdrawn however, if the views recently put forth by Blass on the Western text of the Acts of the Apostles should prove to be correct.*"

Blass, it may be here stated, was an eminent German Professor of Classical Literature, not a theologian or a specialised New Testament critic, who in 1895 edited the Acts in precisely the same impartial spirit in which he had edited other ancient writings, purely as a matter of scientific criticism; and his views are those expressed above in the second section. Blass rests his conclusion on the external and internal evidences equally.

This is enough to shew the importance of the question I am thus, after many years of reflection, endeavouring to bring before readers of the English New Testament for their information and judgment.

5. *Readers of English only are qualified to form a Judgment from the Translation alone*

The question, I repeat, is this. There did exist, and was widely known, from the second century onward, an enlarged text of the Acts which had much in common with D or the Codex Bezæ. This is now admitted by all scholars. This text is commonly described as the Western text, and for brevity and convenience is referred to as the β text. The shorter or Antiochian text is similarly known as the α text. Was the longer text made from the shorter by additions, made by some later unauthorised transcribers, as has been till lately assumed? Or was the shorter text derived from the longer by excisions made by St Luke himself on revision; the excisions being made, it is now suggested, of what could be spared as redundant or unimportant, or for the improvement of style, or as corrections on second thoughts? It is to lay before English readers the internal evidence for the latter hypothesis, furnished by the MS. itself, that this translation is made.

There is obviously no *a priori* improbability in the latter supposition, though it is unfamiliar in New Testament criticism. There have been duplicate original texts in the case of other authors. This general question is not one for Greek and Latin scholars only, though there may be some points on which they may have something special to say; for example, to shew that the additional matter is Lucan in language and literary style; but it appeals to common experience, to the experience of everyone who has written, and then revised, a letter or article or document of any importance.

The reader may now pass on to read carefully this text of the Acts of the Apostles, with the question stated above always present to his mind for judgment: "Does the perusal confirm, or does it not, the suggestion that I am reading a text derived from an early draft of the Acts written by Luke himself; and that on revision and rewriting he struck out the words in thick type, and inserted those within square brackets?"

6. Outline of supplementary matters touched on in this Introduction

The introduction might, as I have suggested, end here. But it is probable that many readers would be assisted by some remarks on the nature of the excisions and additions, and be glad to have their attention drawn to the importance of some of them; and that they would also wish to know something more of the contents and history of this Codex Bezæ; and of the proofs of the early wide circulation of an enlarged and authoritative Western text. They would also probably wish to know something of the origin and reception among scholars of this, at present unfamiliar, view of its importance. The literature of the subject is very extensive, and is being added to every year. I am not attempting to say all that could be said or to give a bibliography of the subject; but only enough to whet the reader's appetite for more.

7. The internal evidence examined. Illustrations of omissions for the sake of brevity

A chief reason for omission in revision appears to be the desire to improve the style by omitting redundancies. Words, therefore, and clauses, that on reading over again seemed superfluous or unimportant are left out. It must be remembered that a roll of papyrus had its limitations of convenient size; and the first and third Gospels and the Acts, even in its shorter form, were perhaps near to that limit. Two or three examples, which I will take from the first few verses of chap. i, will sufficiently illustrate this class of omission, which may be seen in nearly every page.

In i. 2 the β text reads "the apostles whom he had chosen and ordered to proclaim the gospel." In the α text the words "and ordered to proclaim the gospel" do not appear; they were omitted as superfluous.

In i. 4 the β text reads "the promise of the Father which ye heard, saith he, from my mouth." In the α text this is similarly shortened into "which ye heard from me."

In i. 5 the β text reads "Ye shall be baptized with the Holy Ghost, and which ye are about to receive after these not many days until the Pentecost." In the α text this is simplified into "not many days hence."

The words omitted in i. 5 are of considerable value. They explain why "when the day of Pentecost was now come, they were all together in one place," and what they expected.

All these verses are quoted as Scripture by Augustine and others from the β text.

Such omissions are intelligible if made on revision with a view to shorten the text: they are meaningless if regarded as interpolations, or additions.

8. *Interest on various grounds of some of the omitted passages*

Some of the passages struck out on revision, in order to shorten the text, as historically unimportant are of value as shewing the writer's intimate knowledge of the circumstances. They thus have a bearing on questions of date of composition and of authorship. I can find space in this introduction for only a few examples, but the significance of the omitted words must always be considered.

Note for example the frequent excision of notices of time, notices it may be observed very characteristic of St Luke's style. In xvi. 4 the words "at the same time" are struck out. In xvi. 11 "on the morrow," and in xvii. 19 "after some days" are similarly struck out: the last being of some interest as shewing that Paul had been teaching at Athens for some time before they took him to the Areopagus. See also xv. 30, xviii. 19. We may put here the curious excision from xix. 9 that Paul lectured daily in the School of Tyrannus "from eleven o'clock till four."

Such excisions as these notes of time are quite what one would expect from an author who is rewriting and desirous of shortening his own work; but it is difficult to think of them, from the other point of view, as interpolations by later copyists.

Among such omissions, trifling in themselves, is that in xii. 10 in which the β text tells us that, on going out of the prison, Peter and the angel "went down the seven steps," before "passing through one street." A detail like this,

INTRODUCTION 7

however, and the knowledge shewn of Mary's house, and of the citadel, and its stairs, indicate that the writer was well acquainted with Jerusalem.

9. *Instances of some sentences rewritten*

It will be noticed that many passages are more or less rewritten, partly with a view to shorten them, partly from considerations of style. I will give one instance only, from ii. 37. The β text reads "Then all who had come together when they heard this were pricked in their heart, and some of them said to Peter and the apostles, Men and brethren, what therefore shall we do? Shew us." Compare this with our Revised Version taken from the α text. Twenty-eight Greek words have been reduced to eighteen.

There are many such examples of rewriting and compressing or omitting. See v. 39, vi. 10, 11, x. 24–26, xi. 2, xvi. 35–end, xix. 14, xx. 18. Chapters xiv to xxi should be read as a whole in order to give a fair impression.

10. *Excisions few where St Luke appears to be quoting from Documents supplied him*

It is, I think, noticeable that omissions are relatively few and short where St Luke is apparently relying on information, documentary or verbal, obtained from others, as in the early chapters. One such slight excision is of some interest.

In vii. 58 the β text reads "The witnesses laid their garments at the feet of a certain young man whose name was Saul." On revision St Luke omitted the word "certain." Does not this omission imply that St Luke was quoting from a document which had been written before "the young man whose name was Saul" had come to be well known? But when St Luke was writing and revising it seemed out of place so to speak of St Paul. The β text therefore has perhaps preserved a valuable indication, lost in the revision, that the evidence on which St Luke was relying was very early, nearly if not quite contemporary with the facts.

But how impossible that a subsequent copyist should have gratuitously interpolated here the little word "certain"!

11. *Excisions in the account of St Paul's first Missionary Journey, and probable inference*

I have said that the excisions seem to be on a larger scale where St Luke is revising his own personal recollections. This is specially true of his earlier recollections. Note, for example, with this thought in mind, some of the details given in chap. xvi of β, respecting the imprisonment at Philippi of which St Luke was plainly an eye-witness. The narrative in its form in β is very graphic. Or to give slight examples, look at xx. 12. What a touch of reality the story of St Paul's parting from the disciples gains from the little incident that it was "*as they were bidding Paul farewell*" that they brought the young man alive, and were not a little comforted. Or the story of the riot at Ephesus (xix. 28) from the mention that "*they ran into the street.*" What copyist could have thought of interpolating these?

This observation suggests an interesting inference. For if chaps. xiii, xiv, and xv are also read in this text with this thought in mind, it can scarcely fail, I think, to occur to anyone as it did, I think, to Irenæus*, that St Luke may have been with St Paul during part at least of that missionary journey. Even the ordinary text, from xiii. 4 onwards, in its description of the start from Antioch, the visit to Cyprus, the interview with Sergius Paulus, the treatment of Elymas, and the experiences at Perga, the Pisidian Antioch, Iconium, Lystra and Derbe, and the return to the Syrian Antioch, is so graphic and detailed as to assure us that it rests on the testimony, even if it is not itself the description, of an eye-witness. But the β text gives some noteworthy special touches in addition. Note in particular that the proconsul was hearing Barnabas and Saul "with the greatest pleasure" in xiii. 8; and in xiii. 41 how a hush of "silence" fell on all in the Synagogue when St Paul had finished speaking. There is a variation in the β text of xiii. 26 accounted for if St Luke was present. In reporting

* Irenæus describes Luke as inseparable from Paul, and a fellow-workman. See Rendel Harris, *Four Lectures on the Western Text*, p. 88.

St Paul's speech at Antioch (xiii. 26) the β text reads "Brethren, Children of the stock of Abraham, and those among 'us,' who fear God, to us is the word of this salvation sent forth." A similar indication of St Luke's presence was allowed to remain in the α text of xiv. 22 "that through many tribulations 'we' must enter the Kingdom of God." Certainly no other missionary tour of St Paul is related with such detail, except in cases where St Luke was certainly present. Compare the brief accounts given in xv. 41–xvi. 6, xviii. 20–23, xx. 1–3.

If the acceptance of the β text as genuinely Lucan did no more than turn the balance of judgment in favour of St Luke's presence during part at least of this missionary tour, it would enhance not a little the interest of the story.

And, once more, how unlike these little touches and variations are to interpolations by a copyist! We are driven to believe that they were Lucan, and struck out on his revision.

12. *Importance of the fact supplied by this text in Acts xi. 28*

I shall now select the two most important special readings of D, and accepting them as of genuine Lucan authority, indicate some of the inferences to be drawn from them. All that has gone before in this Introduction is only intended to illustrate the internal proof, which the MS. itself furnishes, that these and other statements of the β text must be regarded as unquestionably Lucan, and therefore as the historically valuable words of a contemporary, and as part of our New Testament.

In xi. 28 the β text reads "Now in these days there came down prophets from Jerusalem unto Antioch; and *there was much rejoicing; and when we were gathered together* Agabus spoke, etc." It may be noted that this passage also is quoted in this form by Augustine and others as Scripture. Now the words in italics are omitted in the α text, and they imply that *St Luke was at Antioch at that time*. There is no such implication remaining in the α text. We learn this fact from the β text alone.

There are many points on which this fact throws light.

(*a*) It obviously adds to the probability, spoken of in the last section, of St Luke's having accompanied St Paul on the first missionary tour.

(*b*) It confirms, or it may be a source of, Jerome's statement that St Luke's home was at Antioch, and the similar tradition that Theophilus lived at Antioch.

(*c*) It explains the singular prominence given in the Acts to the affairs of the Church of Antioch. People come to Antioch, and go from Antioch. A whole section of the Acts has its centre at Antioch. It explains St Luke's knowledge of the personnel "in the Church that was there" (xiii. 1) —*i.e.* not mere visitors. We know the names of some of the prophets and teachers there—Barnabas, and Symeon, and Lucius, and Manaen, and Saul. In the list of seven deacons the home of one only is mentioned, Nicolas of Antioch. We know nothing from the Acts of the similar Churches that may have existed in Galilee, and at Samaria, Joppa, Cæsarea, Tyre, Sidon, Damascus, Alexandria, Cyrene, Cilicia (xv. 23 and 41) and must have existed at Jerusalem. This fact brings out the unity and authorship of the book, and throws some light on its purpose. The scope of the writer is limited. Its title in Greek and Latin MSS. is "Acts of Apostles." It does not profess to give an account of the work of the twelve, or a sketch of the growth of the whole Church.

(*d*) It adds considerably to the historic trustworthiness of the details related as to the deputation from Antioch to the Church at Jerusalem to consider the great problem raised by the existence of ardent Gentile Churches, and the resulting decree of the Council. We have here the testimony of one who, if not, as seems probable, actually present, was at least in intimate relation at the time with the chief actors.

(*e*) But there are remoter and very illuminating consequences of our knowing certainly that St Luke was at Antioch at that time. For we read that one of his associates in the Church of Antioch was "Manaen, the *foster-brother*," as the R.V. translates the word, "of Herod the tetrarch." Now Manaen is a most interesting person. Dean Plumptre

INTRODUCTION 11

was, I believe, the first to point out, on the authority of
Josephus, that when Herod the Great was made King of
Judæa, he invited the child (or grandchild) of an old friend
of his, also named Manaen, to come and live at his court,
and be brought up with his own young son, Herod, the
future tetrarch. That child was Manaen. The young Herod
and the young Manaen were brought up as children and
boys together; as youths they visited Greece and Rome
together: and subsequently Manaen lived with Herod at his
court in Tiberias. They were inseparables and intimate
friends during the period of our Lord's public ministry.
It is this Manaen, Herod's foster-brother, who, a very few
years later, appears as one of the prophets or teachers of
the Church at Antioch. How this transformation was
brought about may perhaps be traced.

13. *St Luke's presence at Antioch throws light on one of the sources of his Gospel*

The fact of St Luke's association with Manaen throws
much light on one of the sources of the Gospels. It instantly
explains and confirms St Luke's remarkable knowledge of
occurrences in the court of Herod; such as the help given
to our Lord by Joanna, the wife of Chuza, Herod's steward,
and Susanna (St Luke viii. 3); and the scene (St Luke
xxiii. 8) of our Lord's trial before Herod. From some
source—unless indeed it was pure imagination, like that
of a novelist—St Luke knew not occurrences only, but
motives; he *knew* that "Herod was exceeding glad to see
Jesus"; that he "had been for a long time desirous to see
him"; that "he hoped to have seen some miracle done
by him"; that Herod "questioned him in many words";
that "Herod and Pilate became friends with each other
that very day." Of course it was Manaen, Herod's inseparable, who doubtless was present with Herod, who was
St Luke's informant. Manaen was in fact one of "the eye-
witnesses and ministers of the word" to whom St Luke
refers in his preface (i. 2). Those words exactly describe him.

We shall, of course, not forget that St Mark was also at
Antioch at this time (Acts xii. 25, xiii. 5), nor shall we fail

to see that Manaen was also St Mark's authority for the singularly graphic and accurate account (St Mark vi.14–29) of Herod's birthday feast, of those who were present at it, of the dancing, the oath, the beheading, and the subsequent honourable burial of John "in a tomb" by his disciples; and in particular of the motives and feelings of the principal actors in it. If this is not all sheer romance it must have been supplied by someone present. Who but Manaen?

The early association also of the two evangelists is known only through the β text; and this in itself is of no small interest.

14. *Light is also thrown on St Luke's use of Q and on the history of Manaen*

I am tempted to give another illustration from St Luke's gospel of his knowing some details through Manaen. It is slight, and might easily be overlooked, but it is not the less convincing on that account. St Matthew, in xi. 2 relates an incident thus: "Now when John heard in the prison the works of the Christ he sent by his disciples, and said unto him, Art thou he that should come, etc.?" The same incident is told by St Luke with some additional detail as follows (vii. 18): "The disciples of John told him of all these things. And John calling unto him a certain two of his disciples sent them to the Lord, saying, etc." Now this passage is recognised by all critics as part of an original document, used by St Matthew and St Luke, and by many identified with a collection of our Lord's sayings, reported by an early writer, Papias, to have been made by St Matthew: memoranda in fact, made probably at the time, after the manner of the disciples of a Rabbi. This document, as one of the sources of the first and third gospels, is commonly referred to as Q, standing for Quelle, a source. The form in which it appears in St Matthew is just what we should expect from notes, made by a disciple at the time, of the sayings of our Lord that followed the incident. St Luke had this document before him, and used it largely, as is known. But in this instance he introduced some additional incidents of the story, plainly from the point of view of

John. It was "John's *disciples*," not a mere gaoler, that had told him: he "called *two* of them"—a "*certain*" two, as the Greek has it—which means that St Luke could name them. This information must have come from some disciple of John.

Moreover, it is evident that they were men of high rank, men from the court of Herod: for "as they went their way," as St Matthew puts it, or "when they were departed," as St Luke expresses it, our Lord spoke of the men "clothed in soft raiment" and living "in king's courts." Was not one of the two Manaen? Was not this one of the incidents that led to his becoming an avowed disciple of Christ after the tetrarch's death?

15. *A further inference from St John's Gospel as to the history of Manaen*

I am sure I shall be pardoned for adding one more highly probable conjecture as to information supplied to the Church by Manaen, and a decisive event in his life.

In St John iv. 46–end we read the story of "the nobleman whose son was sick at Capernaum." Nobleman! What a strange title! It is a title unknown to Jew or Greek or Roman. Basilikos! What does it mean? The word plainly puzzled the translators of both our versions. They suggest in the margin "courtier," "ruler," "king's officer." As a title, or description of rank or office, it is, I believe, found nowhere else in Greek literature. It means simply "royal," a royal personage, but not a king. Now what description could be more appropriate for one who was in the unique position of foster-brother and inseparable companion of the king? It is more, I think, than a probable conjecture that Manaen was the "nobleman," the "royal," who besought Jesus "to come down and heal his son."

There are circumstances which support this conjecture, or, as I should prefer to say, confirm this identification. If the conversation with the servants in *vv*. 51, 52 is not sheer invention, it must have come from the "nobleman" himself. The incident also occurred very early in our Lord's Galilæan ministry, for it is mentioned that "this was the second miracle that Jesus did, having come out of Judæa into Galilee." How could a man in high position in the court have heard thus early of Jesus? and heard it on testimony that made him resolve at once to act upon it? He must have heard of Jesus from John the Baptist. Manaen may have been with the "soldiers on service" of St Luke iii. 14 who asked John "And what shall we do?" Manaen would certainly be drawn to the ascetic John by hereditary sympathies, for his father or grandfather, the friend of Herod the Great, was an Essene. Moreover the other miracles related in this gospel were widely attested, notorious. This miracle also would be so if it had occurred to Manaean.

Some such explanation there must be for the manifestly exceptional treatment of John as a prisoner, for the free access to him of his disciples, for the existence at Herod's court of disciples both of John and of Christ, men and women of high position, and for Manaen's early hearing of Jesus. May we not then with reasonable probability trace the conversion of Manaen first to the influence of John the Baptist; then to the interview with Jesus at Cana, and the immediate and simultaneous recovery of his son; then to his again seeing Jesus at work, when he went as one of John's messengers; and finally to his seeing Him before Herod's judgment-seat?

This identification of the "nobleman" of St John's Gospel with Manaen of the Acts is not, however, entirely dependent on the acceptance of the β version of the Acts as Lucan; for St Mark was also associated with Manaen at Antioch; and, indeed, Manaen must have been far too conspicuous a convert in the early Church for his story not to have been widely known. But the completeness of the chain of circumstances that brought Manaen to Christ, and an increase of the feeling that we are throughout in contact with real events, are due to the acceptance of the β text of Acts xi. 28, and are of no little interest and value. We are on solid ground.

16. *Importance of the Bezan Text of the decree of the Council of Jerusalem in Acts xv*

I now pass to the second of the two special readings of D and the β text in general, the omission mentioned above in sections 4 and 12, which is even more important in its results.

INTRODUCTION 15

The ordinary text of xv. 28, 29, gives the decree of the great Council of Jerusalem as follows: "It seemed good to the Holy Ghost and to us to lay upon you no greater burden than these necessary things; that ye abstain from things sacrificed to idols, and from blood, and from things strangled, and from fornication; from which if ye keep yourselves it shall be well with you. Fare ye well." In the β text the opening words are the same; but those that follow are: "that ye abstain from things sacrificed to idols, and from blood, and from fornication; and that whatsoever ye would not should be done to you ye do not to others; from which if ye keep yourselves it shall be well with you. Fare ye well, being sustained by the Holy Spirit." The important point of difference is not the omission in α of the last clauses, interesting as that is; but the absence from β of the words "things strangled," both in this chapter and again in xxi. 25. The questions arise, Which of the texts is really Lucan? or Are both really Lucan? and Which of the two rightly reproduces the text of the decree?

It is now coming to be believed as clearly proved that the β text alone is really Lucan, and alone gives the original and true form of the decree.

17. *The difference of the two texts*

The importance of the difference may not be immediately obvious, but reflection will show that it is very great. For the words "things strangled," if they were in the original text of the decree of the Council, would place it beyond doubt that the Council enacted a food-law for Gentile Christians. It would have declared that no Gentile could be recognised as a member of the Church of Christ unless he observed a Jewish food-law in not eating the flesh of any animal that had been strangled. Moreover, this being plainly a food-law, the prohibition of "blood" was taken to be also a food-law, that blood might not be eaten in any form; and the abstinence from meat which had been offered to idols has also been taken as a food-law. How can the question between the two texts be decided?

18. *The nature of the arguments in support of either text of the decree*

On the one side, in favour of the correctness of the text to which we are all accustomed, is the overwhelming preponderance of the numbers of the MSS. surviving which support it, and among these are the earliest, the fourth-century MSS. If the question is to be decided on the ground of the numbers and antiquity of the MSS. which support the words "things strangled," the β text, which does not include them, has no case.

But, on the other hand, the most ancient testimony other than that of surviving MSS., is as decidedly in favour of the β text. Here we touch on the external evidence. It is the β text that is quoted, Scrivener (Introd. p. lxiii) tells us, "by Irenæus, Tertullian, Cyprian, Ambrose, Pacian, Jerome (who speaks of the omitted words as occurring in some copies), Augustine," and others. It is the β text that was translated into the early Latin, Syriac, and Sahidic and other versions. The β text is used by Ephrem in his commentary*. It is the β text that is assumed in the Apology of Aristides in the middle of the second century. This is of great importance. No proof could be more complete of the wide early acceptance of the β text, and of its admitted authority as Scripture, specially in the West. Some of the Eastern writers quote from the α text. But even Clement of Alexandria is shewn (*Journal of Theol. Studies*, Jan. 1900, p. 292) to have used a text akin to D.

The β text, moreover, of chap. xv, if read as a whole, is even more manifestly than the α text, the work of someone who was either present at the Council, or got his information from those that were. These are very cogent arguments.

19. *Difficulties in accepting the Ordinary Text*

Let us also reflect on some of the difficulties which are involved in accepting the words "things strangled" as having been in the original decree.

There is the incongruity, which must have struck everyone, of coupling with these food-laws the prohibition of

---
* Rendel Harris, *Four Lectures*, p. 27; Chase, *The old Syriac Element*.

INTRODUCTION

fornication, as if it was on a level with them. There is the unaccountable omission of all mention of circumcision, which from xv. 5 we see was the thing chiefly insisted on. There is the inconsistency of saying in the decree that "they would not trouble them which from among the Gentiles turn to God," and then imposing on them food-laws which there is evidence to shew were not generally observed among the Jews of the Dispersion, as seems also to have been admitted by St Peter, xv. 10. There is the statement, in the Bezan text, of Acts xxi. 25, "we sent giving judgment that they should observe nothing of that sort." There is the strange statement in xv. 31 that when the decree was reported at Antioch "the multitude rejoiced for the consolation." There is the still more inexplicable fact that St Paul, shortly afterwards, when the question about the eating of meat "sold in the shambles" (1 Cor. x. 25) which had been offered to idols, does not allude to this decree, while he absolutely forbids (1 Cor. x. 20, 21) sharing in idol feasts. And, finally, there is the fact that no Western Father, or apologist, or hostile critic, ever alludes to such a food-law as enjoined on Christians. If it ever existed it was ignored from the first.

That such a food-law should have formed part of the decree is, on such grounds as these, so incredible, that critics have always regarded this chapter as their chief support for denying the early date and Lucan authorship of at least this part of the Acts. Harnack, for example, who up to 1899 accepted the a text as giving the original form of the decree, wrote that "the statement was so inconsistent with facts that to suppose the writer to have been a companion of St Paul was quite inadmissible."

20. *Difficulties removed by accepting the Text in this Codex as the true report of the Decree*

From such reasoning as this critics have been of late led to the conclusion that the β text gives the true form of the decree. For if the words "things strangled" were not in the decree, the natural interpretation of the decree, would, beyond all question, have been that it forbade the three great sins of *idolatry*, *murder*, and *fornication*; and was in fact a purely moral law: *idolatry*, of which the outward expression was sharing in the "sacramental communion with the idol," the temple feast, which St Paul describes (1 Cor. x. 18–22) as "communion with devils"; *murder*, commonly spoken of as blood-shedding or blood, as in St Matt. xxiii. 35 and often in the Septuagint; and *fornication*. These are the crimes forbidden to all Gentile Christians by the decree; associated here as in Rev. xxii. 15, "Without are the fornicators, and the murderers, and the idolaters." The decree was a simple moral law, summarised, emphasised and consecrated by the quotation of our Lord's words from the Sermon on the Mount, naturally thrown into the negative form—"Whatsoever ye would not that should be done to you ye do not to others." This might well be hailed with joy everywhere. It was the final emancipation of Christianity from Judaism. Christianity had never been bound to the temple and the Sacrificial priesthood of the Jews. Now it was publicly transformed from a tribal or national religion to one that was universal; and the declaration is that the mark of the universal religion was to be faith in Christ's Revelation of God, along with morality and the observance of the golden rule.

The acceptance of the β text shews the greatness of the Council of Jerusalem. Well may Harnack say, "The Scribe who first wrote the little word 'strangled' opposite 'blood' on the margin of his exemplar created a flood, which has for almost 2000 years swamped the correct interpretation of the whole passage....We can close whole libraries of commentaries and investigations, as documents of the history of a gigantic error!...The importance of Codex D (Bezæ)—supported to be sure by all the Western authorities—is here brought into great prominence."

21. *The words "things strangled" a later Interpolation unknown to the earliest Texts*

But how did the words "things strangled" get into the α or Antiochian text? This is not known. Harnack offers the conjecture given in the last section; that it was a mistaken explanation of the word "blood," put by someone in

INTRODUCTION

the margin of a MS., and regarded by some subsequent copyist as denoting an accidental omission, and by him inserted in the text itself. Additions to the author's text have sometimes originated in this way. Or it may have been a deliberate interpolation on the part of someone of "the sect of the Pharisees who believed," who wished to get apostolic authority for insisting on this part of the ceremonial law. This suggestion receives some support from the significant omissions in the later text of Acts xxi. 25. The β text there makes it clear that the decree was that the Gentiles were to observe nothing of the Jewish Ceremonial: "we sent giving judgment that they should observe nothing of that sort except to guard themselves from idol sacrifices, and from blood and from fornication." But, whatever its origin may have been, we may now feel sure that the Apostolic Council guaranteed for ever the Gentile Churches entire freedom from Jewish ceremonial law. This is in accordance with history. The Church from the first understood the Apostolic document as an ethical rule. Jewish morality was to be insisted on as a law of God; but Jewish ceremonial was not.

22. *The Evidences internal and external for the view here advocated cumulative and convincing*

I have now given a sketch of the internal evidence from the omissions made in rewriting the β text that it is of Lucan authorship, and some of the important results that follow from accepting it as such. This is the main point; which the reader will, I think, after due study, come to regard as finally established.

But this leads me to repeat that the grounds for so accepting it are only outlined and illustrated in this Introduction. No one can appreciate the full force of the cumulative internal evidence till he has read the whole text, and satisfied himself that of the numerous excisions, short or long, all are explicable on the hypothesis that an author is revising and somewhat shortening his own work, and that most of these omitted words or phrases are so superfluous, and so entirely free from any doctrinal tendency, as to make it extremely unlikely, to say the least, that any copyist should have thought it worth his while to interpolate them. The rewritten passages also lead to the same conclusion. On comparing them no one, I think, can bring himself to believe that the β text is derived from rewriting the α.

It will, of course, be understood that the Bezan texts which we possess were copied from older MSS., which in their turn were copied from others; and that our Greek text has thus been subjected to many influences, and does not exactly reproduce the text as it left St Luke's hand. It is well, however, to remember Hort's saying that the doubtful words scarcely exceed one-thousandth of the whole N.T.: and we may feel sure that the substance of this text is Lucan. To discover the most probable underlying text or, in this case, texts is the highly skilled work of the textual critic.

The external evidence also, derived from ancient references to the β text, and from its use in early versions—the evidence which converted Harnack—must be carefully weighed. But this I am not called to expound in detail here, or to enforce.

23. *Confirmed by minor verbal alterations, and an avoidance in the revision of over statement*

There is a class of minor differences between the two texts, in which one word is substituted for another, which is in most cases a synonym. These changes are in general, I suppose, matters of style or rhythm; as if an English writer on revision preferred "he beheld" to "he saw": or "he went away" to "he departed thence." I do not reproduce these minor changes except in a few instances.

But there is one change of a word, which I have not seen noticed, which is of considerable interest. It is not a change to a synonym, and it suggests careful and scientific accuracy on the part of St Luke. In v. 15, 16, after the account of their laying sick people in the street so that the shadow of Peter might fall on them as he passed by, the β text continues: "for they were set free from every sickness which each one of them had"; and goes on to say that all who were brought into Jerusalem were "cured." Both these statements were, it may be assumed, in the authority from which St Luke is quoting: and he inserted them in his first draft. But on revision and rewriting I imagine that he felt this to be an over-statement. He therefore left out the first clause altogether; and instead of a word which means "cured" he used a word which strictly means "attended to," "relieved," "medically treated." I must explain that there are two Greek words, not really synonymous, though sometimes they may be loosely used as such; and both are translated in our versions "healed" or "cured," which, I suppose, mean the same thing. But St Luke was a physician, and uses them accurately. He observes the distinction. He perhaps knew Galen's maxim quoted by Harnack, that "a physician ought first to *cure* his own symptoms, and then attempt to *treat* those of others." In Acts xxviii. 8, 9, the distinction is marked. St Luke tells us that St Paul *cured* the father of Publius, and that the rest of the people who had diseases in the island came and were "*medically treated*"; by St Luke doubtless as well as by St Paul, for he writes that "they honoured *us* with many honours." But in St Luke's Gospel (ix. 11) he writes differently of our Lord, and says that "them that had need of medical treatment (or relief) he *cured*." The alteration of the word, therefore, in St Luke's revision of Acts v. 16 is significant. It may be noted that St Luke uses the word "attended to" in Acts xvii. 25, where the revisers translate it "served." "Neither is God '*served*' by men's hands as though he needed anything." The same word is so used by Plato, and we ourselves speak of Divine *service*. It is to be regretted, I think, that the revisers did not see their way to mark this distinction.

24. *Confirmed further by the additions made by St Luke in the revision*

Besides the *excisions* from the draft, shewn by thick type in the version that follows, and besides the rewriting of some passages not so easily shewn in detail, and besides the occasional change of a word into a synonym, not generally indicated at all, there are *additions* made in the revised, or *a* text, shewn by square brackets.

These are much less numerous than the excisions, and of less importance; but so far as they go they will be seen to be consistent with, and indeed to confirm, the hypothesis of revision by the author. In most cases they are very slight, and seem to be purely literary, in order to link the sentences better, or to prevent a misapprehension. See, for example, iv. 14, 15, 17 and xi. 7, 9, 12, 17. In some cases it is to make a quotation more full, or to give the reference, as in ii. 16–20. In a few cases the addition is of some significance. In xvii. 18, after "he seemeth to be a setter forth of strange gods," the addition of the words "because he preached unto them Jesus and the resurrection" seems to be an explanation of the plural "gods," and to suggest that some of his hearers thought that the Anastasis or resurrection preached by St Paul was a goddess.

25. *Some supplementary information*

I have now finished this outline of the internal evidence that is furnished by the version itself as to its being derived from St Luke's first draft of the book, written prior to the revision from which the α text has been derived.

The reader will now probably wish to know something more about the Codex Bezæ itself; its nature, date and history, the views that have been entertained by critics as to its textual and historical value, and in particular the origin and reception of the view lately revived by Blass which I am advocating in this Introduction. But these subjects lie outside the scope of this little work. I am not writing a critical account of the Codex. I have already said that I wish to give only enough to whet the reader's appetite for more.

The completest account of this MS., of its history, collations, and editions, and of the critical problems it raises, down to the date 1864, is contained in the Introduction to Scrivener's edition of the Codex (*Bezæ Codex Cantabrigiensis*, edited with a critical introduction, annotations and facsimiles, by Frederick H. Scrivener, M.A. (Deighton, Bell and Co., 1864)). This work is indispensable to anyone who wishes to study the subject critically. In that Introduction of 64 quarto pages of small print he gives all the facts known prior to that date with marvellous accuracy, a minute examination of its variations from the α text, and of the changes and comments made by later scribes, "some ten or twelve in number"; and this is followed by the full text of the MS. and notes. But a very brief outline of some matters may here be given.

26. *A brief description of the Codex Bezæ*

The Codex Bezæ is a MS. volume, written on vellum, its pages being 10 inches high and 8 inches broad. Each page contains 33 lines. The letters are all capitals, those of the Latin very like the Greek; the words in general not divided from one another by a space. The left-hand page, the page of honour, is the Greek text D; the right-hand page is the Latin d. The volume originally contained the four Gospels, placed in the usual Western order, Matthew, John, Luke, Mark (the apostles having precedence), The Acts of the Apostles, and the Catholic Epistles. But a considerable number of leaves are missing. In the Acts are missing viii. 29 to x. 14; xxi. 2–10, 16–18; xxii. 10–20; and all that follow xxii. 29, about a quarter of the whole book. Many leaves are in bad condition, and some passages wholly or quite illegible.

The text is divided into lines of curiously different lengths or *stichoi*, a division shewn by Scrivener to be copied from older MSS., and more carefully copied in the Acts than in some of the Gospels. The division is evidently literary, in order to assist the reader and the listener. This will be best seen by an example. I take Acts xvii. 11:

"Some therefore of them believed,
But some did not believe:
And of the Greeks and of those of honourable estate,
Both men and women,
Many believed.
But when those from Thessalonica knew,
Jews, that the word of God was proclaimed
At Berœa, and that they believed,
They came also thither, and there stirring up
And troubling the multitude, did not cease."

The number of letters in a line in the Greek text ranges from eight in Acts xiii. 16, to forty-four in xiii. 31.

Scrivener gives three pages of facsimile; and these, and his introduction, shew that the MS. has passed through many hands, not fewer than twelve, of correctors and others, who made erasions and interlinear corrections, and also added liturgical notes in the margin as to the lessons read in the Church services. The lines and text of the Latin and Greek in general correspond.

The volume was presented to the University of Cambridge on 6 Dec. 1581 by Theodore Beza, the well-known French Reformer, and is now preserved in the University Library. Scrivener gives a list of its collations and editions prior to his own; and in 1899 the University of Cambridge published a magnificent photographic facsimile of the whole MS. This edition was reviewed by Mr (now Sir) F. G. Kenyon of the British Museum in the *Journal of Theological Studies* for Jan. 1900. He there discusses the date and country in which it was probably written. The handwriting he describes as rough and irregular; and though a date in the sixth century is regarded as more probable, evidence which pushed it into the fifth century would be accepted without difficulty. He considers that the most probable birthplace of the MS., *i.e.* the place where it was copied from an older manuscript, was Southern Gaul, the Church of the Greek Missionaries Pothinus and Irenæus of about A.D. 170. The liturgical notes shew that the Greek text was used in the services. Both the Latin and Greek texts are full of grammatical mistakes and mis-spellings, and shew that the writer was not familiar with the correct forms of these languages; they indicate country and dialect uses, rather than a literary centre as the origin of the MS. The Latin appears to be the vernacular or rustic Latin, as it was passing into the spoken language of the South of France in the fifth century. It should be added that Professor Burkitt has subsequently given good reasons in the *Journal of Theological Studies* for assigning the MS. to the fifth century.

Its history prior to 1581 is not known: but there is good reason for surmising that it was part of the plunder of the

INTRODUCTION   25

city of Lyons in 1562, and in particular of the monastery
there of St Irenæus; and that it was given to Beza. He
speaks of it as "found" there when the civil war broke out
in 1562. "Outward appearance," says Scrivener, "and
internal indications, point to Gaul as the native country
of Codex Bezæ, nor is there any reason for thinking that it
ever left that country till it was carried into Italy in 1546,
for reference at the Council of Trent."

*27. The origin of the hypothesis that there were two
Lucan originals of MSS. of the Acts of the Apostles*

The history of the hypothesis that St Luke wrote two
copies of the Acts, and that D is derived from the earlier,
which was also the longer, is briefly as follows:

A French scholar, Jean Le Clerc (born 1657), after study-
ing the unique peculiarities of this Codex, suggested, early in
the eighteenth century, as a probable but novel explanation
of them, that St Luke made two copies of the Acts, and
that while all other existing Greek MSS., which had up to
that time been collated, had been made from one, Codex
Bezæ alone was derived from the other. This hypothesis
was, I have read, supported by a Dutch scholar, Hemster-
huis, but by no one else, and it dropped out of sight.

The suggestion was made, whether independently or not
I do not know, in 1848 by a German scholar, Bornemann,
that Luke kept a private diary in which he noted doings
of the apostles; that the diary was afterwards found, and
extracts from it inserted in some copies. He afterwards
thought that D was Luke's original work; and he further
shewed that the shorter text was derived from the longer
by excision, and not the longer from the shorter by interpolation. His papers attracted little attention, and once
more the suggestion dropped out of sight. It may perhaps
have been felt that the suggestion was difficult to harmonize
with the belief universally held of Divine verbal inspiration
of Scripture.

Again, in 1895, a well-known German classical scholar,
Blass, re-examined the whole question in the light of the
very much more extensive and accurate knowledge of MSS.

and versions and quotations then available; and he came to the same conclusion; adding that the original copy was probably retained at Rome, and that copies of it circulated widely in the West, while the revised copy was sent to Theophilus at Antioch, and its copies were circulated in the East.

But Blass went much further than his predecessors were able to do. He attempted to reconstruct the Western text of the Acts, using for that purpose all the other sources of information as to that early text that I spoke of in Section 18, the result of another half-century of keen and widespread study and collation of texts. The two texts of Codex Bezæ, it must be remembered, though the chief are not the sole authority for the early Western text. He used the others, of which he gives a list, not only to supply the text where some leaves of D are missing, but conjecturally to correct errors in D. Variations in the Western text appeared early. For example, in ii. 9 for Judæa Jerome quotes Syria, and Tertullian Armenia. Blass's conjectures have naturally been disputed, as will be seen in the article in the *Encyclopædia Biblica* quoted in Section 4, and in some cases probably with success. But no one has, I believe, shaken his main contention. The reconstruction of the Western text is still an unaccomplished work. The ripest scholarship, the widest knowledge of ancient versions and commentaries, and the devotion of years will be needed for this text.

28. *Why the ordinary text is preserved in so many MSS. and this text became so rare*

It is an obvious question why, if the β text was so widely circulated and had such authority in the earliest centuries, the MSS. that preserved it should have so largely disappeared. This question is partly answered by Westcott and Hort (*N.T.* vol. II. p. 142, ed. 1881), and to this volume I refer the reader. It is certain that the β text was widely circulated in the earliest centuries, and that it survived long in the West. Bede's quotations from the Acts for example, shew that he used that text; and King Alfred's Preface to his laws contains a plain quotation from the β text of the Council of Jerusalem.

INTRODUCTION 27

The rarity of surviving Western MSS. may be connected with the earlier date of monachism and monastic libraries in the East than in the West, and with their somewhat greater immunity from pillage. Few indeed are the fragments of English MSS. of the New Testament that have survived from the early days of the English Church*.

But it was to some extent an accident that the unknown MSS. used by Cardinal Ximenes for the Complutensian Text in 1514, and the three or four MSS. which Erasmus used for his Greek Testament (1515–1535), and which thus formed the basis of the text of our Authorised Version, were of the α type; and somewhat of an accident that the oldest surviving MSS., the Sinaitic, and Vatican and Alexandrian, and Codex Ephræmi are all of the same type.

29. *Were there also two original Lucan Texts of his Gospel?*

The question will naturally be asked whether the MS. of St Luke's Gospel in Codex Bezæ may also be regarded as derived from a first draft, and to be truly Lucan. I have not studied this question at all, and offer no opinion, and I do not know whether it has been recently examined. But there are interesting variations in this MS. of St Luke's Gospel which suggest that it is a not impossible hypothesis.

For example, there is the well-known saying attributed to our Lord, usually placed among the uncanonical agrapha. It occurs in vi. 5. After the words "He said unto them, The Son of man is lord of the sabbath," D adds "On the same day seeing someone working on the sabbath, he said to him, Man, if thou knowest what thou art doing blessed art thou; but if thou knowest not, thou art cursed and a transgressor of the law." St Luke may have thought on revision that this was probably incorrectly reported, and had better be omitted.

And in xiii. 7–9 there may be an instance of rewriting in order to improve the style. D reads: "Behold it is three years since I have come seeking fruit on this fig-tree and I

* But see Westcott and Hort, II. Chap. ii. Section C. Ed. 1881.

find none. Bring the axe. Cut it down. Why does it cumber the ground? But he answering saith to him, Lord, let it alone this year also till I shall dig about it, and throw on it a basket of dung; and if it bear fruit, well, but if not for the future thou shalt cut it down."

In xvi. 19 D reads, before the parable of Dives and Lazarus, "And he spake also another parable."

And there is at least one little touch in D which must have come from an eye-witness, in xxiii. 42, where, of the dying robber on the cross, the text in D reads "And, *turning to the Lord*, he said to him, Lord, remember me in the day of thy kingdom." The question calls for careful examination.

The variations in D in St Mark's Gospel from the common text are few and unimportant. In St Matt. i. 16, xx. 28, xxv. 1 and St John vi. 56 are a few words supported by old authorities; and D is the oldest Greek MS. which preserves the undoubtedly genuine, if not Johannine, passage vii. 53–viii. 11. These Gospels offer no parallel to the variations in the text of the Acts. They indicate, however, that D was derived from some ancient source.

30. *Why this view of the value of the text in Codex Bezæ was not adopted by the Revisers in* 1880

There is another, and very interesting question, which is sure to occur to the reader—Why so satisfactory and simple a solution of the problem of the curious variations in Codex Bezæ was not accepted by that company of eminent scholars and critics who were in 1870 entrusted by Convocation with the duty of preparing a Revised Version of the New Testament.

The real answer may be that the suggestions put forward by Le Clerc, and Borneman, mentioned above in Section 27, were not present to their minds. They had dropped out of sight. And it must be remembered that the work of Blass had not then been written.

But a sufficient reason is given in the Revisers' Preface to the New Testament, to which I refer the reader. It will be there seen that among the "Principles and Rules" for

INTRODUCTION 29

the revisers were (1) that they were to introduce as few alterations as possible into the text of the Authorised Version consistently with faithfulness; (4) that the text to be adopted was to be that for which the evidence was decidedly preponderating; and (5) that they were to make no change in the text except on the approval of two-thirds of the revisers present. It cannot be doubted that in 1880 the evidence for the α text decidedly preponderated.

31. *Professor Hort's Study of the Texts of the New Testament of great value*

At that time the highest authorities on the text of the New Testament were Westcott and Hort, and in particular the latter. They published in 1881 a carefully revised text of the New Testament in two volumes; the Introduction to which fully and clearly explains their principles and methods. It will, I think, be long before that Introduction is out of date. They were fully aware of the existence and antiquity and authority of the Western text, and of its peculiarities, as the following quotations shew; but, as far as I can remember, the suggestion of there having been two Lucan originals does not seem to have been present to their minds. It had dropped out of sight.

In vol. I. p. 544, they clearly state that the textual value of a MS. depends not on its own antiquity, nor on the number of its supporters, but on the authority of its earliest traceable progenitor. "One early document," they write, "may have left a single descendant, another a hundred or a thousand:...No available presumptions...can be obtained from number alone, that is, from number not as yet interpreted by descent."

On p. 547 they write: "A text virtually identical with the prevalent Greek text of the Middle Ages was used by Chrysostom and other Antiochian Fathers in the latter part of the fourth century." But they go on to say that "...The writings of Origen, which carry us to the middle of the third century, and even earlier, establish the prior existence of at least 3 types of text....The most clearly marked of these is one that has long been conventionally known as 'Western.'" And again (I. 548): "The rapid and wide propagation of the Western text is the most striking phenomenon of textual history in the three centuries following the death of the Apostles. The first clear evidence (Marcion, Justin) shews us a text containing definitely Western readings before the middle of the second century. ...The text used by all the Ante-Nicene Greek writers not connected with Alexandria (Irenæus, etc.) is substantially Western. Even in the two chief Alexandrians, Clement and Origen, especially in some of Origen's writings, Western quotations hold a conspicuous place, while in Eusebius they are on the whole predominant....The Old Latin Versions were Western from the first....The Old Syriac, and every ancient version, was affected by it."

It is plain that Dr Hort was perfectly familiar with all the relevant facts then known. Could anyone have urged the claims of the Western text on external grounds more effectively? But the explanation now before us of the perplexing facts seems never to have occurred to him. He writes of the Codex D on page 548, "The chief and constant characteristic is a love of paraphrase....Words and even clauses are changed, omitted, and inserted with surprising freedom....Readiness to adopt alterations or additions from sources extraneous to the books which ultimately became canonical. These various tendencies must have been in action for some time." But he comforts himself with the remark that "the Western licence did not prevail everywhere, and MSS. unaffected by its results were still copied."

On p. 554 he inadvertently, if we may venture to use such a word of anything Dr Hort ever wrote, speaks of the Western text as containing "interesting matter *omitted* in the other Pre-Syrian texts, yet manifestly *not due to the inventiveness of scribes.*" He speaks of them on p. 565 as "come from an extraneous source."

How close he was to the answer to the riddle! How he would have welcomed it!

INTRODUCTION 31

32. *Scrivener's final remarks on the Greek Text of the Codex Bezæ*

No one in any age has studied the Codex with so wide a knowledge and such accuracy as Mr Scrivener. His final remarks are therefore of great value. He wrote in 1864 as follows (p. lxiv). After speaking of the Latin text of the Codex and its date and origin he proceeds: "The Greek text, on the other hand, we believe to bear distinct traces of an origin far more remote. Itself immediately derived from a Manuscript whose stichometry was arranged just like its own (see p. xxiii) it must ultimately be referred to an *exemplar* wherein the verses, now so irregular and confused, were first distributed according to an orderly system (see p. xvii), and such an original would most likely belong to the third century at the latest. In respect, moreover, to its rare and peculiar readings, the close resemblance of Codex Bezæ to the text of the Syriac versions (with which it could hardly have been compared later than the second century), and to that of the old Latin, yet unrevised by Jerome, as employed by Cyprian and Augustine in Africa, by the translator of Irenæus, by Hilary, and Lucifer and Ambrose in the North-West—such resemblance (far too common to be the result of chance) persuades us to regard with the deepest interest this venerable monument of Christian learning; inasmuch as the modification of the inspired writings which it preserves, whatever critics may eventually decide respecting its genuineness and purity, was at once widely diffused and largely received by the holiest men in the best ages of the Primitive Church."

Scrivener wrote, of course, before the time of Blass; he was, however, acquainted with Bornemann's work mentioned above in Section 27: but, like Tischendorf, he seems not to have treated it very seriously. Tischendorf doubted whether it was not written as a jest. Scrivener retained the traditional view that "the characteristic feature of Codex D was its perpetual tendency to interpolation, its adding to the received text." But that he felt this explanation inadequate he shews in many ways. He speaks, for example, of these additions as "whether genuine or spurious." His view is, in fact, not inconsistent with that of Blass. But his chief aim was to shew, by constant detailed comparison with ancient versions and early writers, that the Greek text of Codex Bezæ, as it stands, is in the main identical with the text that was current, both in the East and West as early as the second century. And this aim he achieved, and it is a result of the first importance, for the text could not have won such wide currency so early unless it possessed strong claims for genuineness.

33. *Why recent opinions of Scholars are not here summarized*

I purposely do not quote such opinions as I happen to know of more recent and living authorities on textual criticism of the New Testament. It is partly because I am not in a position to do so at all completely: any selection that I could give of names of such British and American, and *a fortiori* of German, French and Dutch scholars, would be imperfect and therefore misleading. But the main reason is that the new light enlarges and strengthens the external evidence for the early date and value of a Western text with which I am not here concerned. The question I deal with here is the internal evidence; and it is largely a literary, and even commonsense, question. I am, however, aware that in Great Britain the subject has not as yet attracted the general attention which I am sure it deserves.

34. *Grounds on which late dates have often been assigned by critics to the writings usually regarded as Lucan*

In Section 4 of this Introduction I quoted the words of a leading and representative scholar, Dr P. S. Schmiedel, in which he stated that his conclusions as to the late date (A.D. 105–130) to be assigned to the Acts would have to be withdrawn if Blass's views were accepted. Harnack has similarly altered his date, and names A.D. 57 to 59. This change of assigned dates is so great and so surprising as to be scarcely intelligible until it is understood how the main arguments for the late date are not only met but removed by the β text. The reader may naturally ask What are these arguments? Why should anyone doubt that the date of completing the writing of the book was the end of the two years of St Paul's imprisonment at Rome (Acts xxviii. 30)? If written later, why is there no mention or hint of any subsequent event?

The reader must be referred to Schmiedel's article in the *Encyclopædia Biblica* and similar works. I cannot pretend to do the arguments justice; for I do not feel that they carry much, if any, weight. But perhaps the following, though very brief, is not an unfair sketch of them.

1. If the ordinary text of the decree of the Council of Jerusalem is that of the original writer it is so inconsistent with historical facts that it could not have been written by any contemporary.

This is weighty: but it is removed altogether if the β text is accepted, as has been shewn above, and as is admitted by Schmiedel.

2. It is certain that the Acts was written after the Gospel of St Luke. But in chap. xxi of that Gospel a prediction is attributed to our Lord of the details of the siege of Jerusalem under Titus, which correspond, it is urged, too precisely to the facts to have been a prediction. The Gospel, it is argued, was therefore written after A.D. 70; and the Acts still later.

On this I would refer the reader to Knowling's Introduction to his edition of the Acts in the *Expositor's Bible*. But I may remark that this argument carries little weight with those who note that our Lord plainly had Daniel chap. ix in mind; and also bear in mind that such events were regarded as probable long before they took place. Knowling quotes other instances of prediction; and, I think, it was Blass who remarked that it was harder for Savonarola to predict a Luther, than for Christ to predict a Titus.

3. There are passages in St Luke's writings which may indicate an acquaintance with Josephus. This is a very precarious argument.

4. But the fundamental reason for insisting on a late date is perhaps the half-conscious *a priori* conviction that no contemporary evidence for events outside the familiar order of nature, and in particular for the unexplained phenomena attending the resurrection of our Lord, is possible. It is first assumed that the events related did not really happen. Time must, therefore, be allowed for legends to grow up, invented to support a belief which had no real historical foundation: and therefore, it is argued, that Gospels and the Acts *must* be late products of Christian piety indeed, but also of Christian credulity. And it seems to me that some critics, to whom it would be absurd to attribute any such prepossessions, are so anxious not to allow themselves to be prejudiced in the opposite sense, that they underestimate the obvious and clear arguments for an early date.

35. *Brief statement of results which follow from acceptance of the views above advocated*

Finally, it remains that I should state somewhat more explicitly the general results of accepting the Bezan text of the Acts as even more purely Lucan and historical than the Antiochian text; though it is certainly far less free than the best Antiochian texts from trifling errors of transcription, and what is known as conflation.

It will put an end to the long disputes over the authorship and date of the Acts. We shall hear no more of the Acts being non-Lucan in compilation or authorship, and no more of such dates for it as A.D. 110 to 130, or even of A.D. 80 or 70. The obstacles that made scholars hesitate to accept the obvious arguments for an early date have been removed. This is the primary result; and it is of the first importance, because it carries with it such weighty consequences.

It would be foreign to my purpose, and take too much space, to do more here than barely indicate those obvious arguments, but some such summary may be useful. For a thorough presentation of them I would refer the reader to a paper by the Rev. R. Rackham in the *Journal of Theological Studies* for October 1899.

INTRODUCTION

It is surely impossible that a writer who had described so fully St Paul's defence before his Roman provincial judges at Cæsarea, and their treatment of his cause, could, if the subsequent trial before the Emperor Nero had taken place, have omitted to mention it. To tell in detail the story of an appeal, made many years previously, and not even to allude to the result, is a literary impossibility. It would be to tell a well-planned story, and omit its climax.

Perhaps it may be said in reply that the writer contemplated a third and later volume which was to report the climax. Yes: but the tone, the presentiments, of vol. II. could not fail to be affected by the writer's knowledge of that climax, whether it was St Paul's martyrdom, or his liberation, had it already taken place. It is impossible that the atmosphere of the years before the trial and before the overthrow of Jerusalem could have been, by any dramatic effort, reproduced after it. Compare the peaceful close of the Acts, written before these events, and the lurid passionate tone of some chapters in the Revelation. Or think of the account in the Acts of St Paul's last visit to Jerusalem, with all going on as usual. Could that have been written years after the Temple and city had been destroyed, the nation scattered, and the Church of Christians no longer there? Impossible! And how disproportionate in detail if written many years later, would be the last few chapters!

The whole position had altered completely between A.D. 60 and A.D. 80, not to speak of A.D. 130. When the Acts was being written the questions at issue were still the relations between Pharisaic and Gentile Christians, about Hellenists and proselytes, about the recognition of a Gentile Christianity as possible. But by A.D. 80 those questions had been settled. When the Acts was being written the Jews were persecuting the Christian Gentiles: but by A.D. 80 both Jews and Christians were alike the object of persecution. When the Acts was being written there were hopes that Christianity would be soon, through the appeal to Nero, a permitted religion in the empire: by A.D. 80 it had been decided that it was not permitted.

It is argued that there are inconsistencies between the

narrative of the Acts and some of St Paul's Epistles. But both are incomplete accounts, and the apparent inconsistencies might disappear if we knew the whole story, and allowance made for failure of knowledge and memory. And the inconsistencies are proofs that the writer of the Acts had not before him copies of the Epistles. No later writer on the Acts of the Apostles would have failed to consult them.

The Bezan text contributes much, as the reader of it will see, to the impression the book conveys of personal knowledge: there are frequent touches of colour in the narrative which, in combination with manifest simplicity and truthfulness, are impossible in anyone but a contemporary and eye-witness.

The net result of such considerations, of the correctness of which the Bezan text supplies the final assurance, is that the Acts was written about A.D. 57 to 59, at Rome. But this throws back the date of the Gospel of St Luke, say to A.D. 56 or 57, when St Luke was at Cæsarea and its neighbourhood, and could gather and test his materials. And even then "many had taken in hand to draw up narratives" of Christ's words and actions. One of these many was doubtless his friend and old companion St Mark, whose Gospel is thus thrown back to at least an early date in the sixth decade of the century.

And behind the gospels is the document Q, imbedded, but discernible, in the Gospels of St Matthew and Luke. It bears the marks of a still earlier time. We have good authority for believing that St Matthew made a collection of our Lord's sayings. It may be identified with Q. A late great Bishop of Manchester, Dr Moorhouse, a most careful student of New Testament criticism, wrote to me—the letter is published in his life—"that the most serious reason for doubting whether we have not in document Q a contemporary report of our Lord's teaching is that it is almost too good news to be true. What a relief it would be to feel that in about one-third of the contents of St Matthew we have—without doubt, and without the admixture of traditional accretions—the very words of our Lord."

I know that we must beware of prejudices, of making the wish the father to the thought. But we are not bound to say that any hypothesis or conclusion is too good to be true, if the evidence for it is convincing.

And among the collateral evidences for the early dates of the historic documents of our faith, and among the glimpses obtainable of the firsthand sources from which they were derived, and for preserving the only true record of the momentous decision of the great Council of Jerusalem, the Magna Charta of the Church, the text of the Acts of the Apostles preserved in the Codex Bezæ holds a unique place.

Finally, the acceptance of these early dates is an indication that one stage of New Testament criticism is ending, and another beginning. We have for many decades past watched the evaporation under criticism of certain elements in the New Testament narratives. We are now beginning to witness the crystallisation of the solid and imperishable residue.

II

NOTE ON THE TRANSLATION THAT FOLLOWS

THE sole object of publishing this translation of the Greek text of so much of the Acts of the Apostles as has survived in the Codex Bezæ is to enable the English reader to form a judgment, based on internal and literary evidence alone, as to the relation between the original source of this text, and that of the shorter text from which our A.V. and R.V. are translated. It is my belief that a careful examination of it will do more than suggest to the reader as possible, it will convince him of the fact, that we have before us traces of the revision of a work by the author himself, the words in thick type being struck by him out of his first draft, and the words in square brackets introduced. The other argument, based on external and historical evidence, pointing to the same conclusion, is also briefly alluded to in the Introduction.

This being the sole object of the translation, it will, I hope, be understood that this is not a critical collation of texts, and deals with no other critical question. Many obvious errors of transcription in the MS. are tacitly corrected. In some rewritten passages the whole is in thick type though parts of them appear in the ordinary text. The reader is assumed to have the R.V. open before him, or in his memory. The translation is in general that of the R.V. or its margin.

I have, in a word, endeavoured to put before the English reader the purely literary question—revision by author or interpolation by copyist—in a form at once fair and simple and readable.

The translation was made partly from Kipling's facsimile in folio, and completed and revised from Scrivener's very careful transcription. I fear that some errors will have been made or escaped correction, and I shall be truly grateful to anyone who will send me a note of them.

III

Chapter I

1,2 THE former treatise I made, O Theophilus, concerning all that Jesus began both to do and to teach, until the day in which he was received up, after that he had given commandment through the Holy Spirit unto the apostles whom he had chosen, **and ordered to proclaim the**
3 **gospel:** to whom he also shewed himself alive after his passion by many proofs, appearing unto them by the space of forty days, and speaking the things concerning the king-
4 dom of God: and, being assembled together with them, he charged them not to depart from Jerusalem, but to wait for the promise of the Father, which ye heard, **saith he,**
5 **from my mouth:** for John indeed baptized with water; but ye shall be baptized with the Holy Spirit, **and which ye are about to receive** after these not many days **until the Pentecost.**
6 They therefore, when they were come together, asked him, saying, Lord, dost thou at this time restore the king-
7 dom of Israel? And he said unto them, It is not for you to know times or seasons, which the Father hath set within
8 his own authority. But ye shall receive power, when the Holy Spirit is come upon you; and ye shall be my witnesses both in Jerusalem, and in all Judæa and Samaria, and unto
9 the uttermost part of the earth. And when he had said these things, [as they were looking], a cloud received him,
10 and he was taken away out of their sight. And while they were looking stedfastly into heaven as he went, behold, two
11 men stood by them in white apparel; which also said, Ye men of Galilee, why stand ye looking into heaven? this Jesus, which was received up from you [into heaven], shall so come in like manner as ye beheld him going into heaven.

12 Then returned they unto Jerusalem from the mount called Olivet, which is nigh unto Jerusalem, a sabbath day's journey off.

13 And when they were come in, they went up into the upper chamber, where they were abiding; both Peter and John, [and] James and Andrew, Philip and Thomas, Bartholomew and Matthew, James of Alphæus, [and] Simon the
14 Zealot, and Judas of James. These all with one accord continued stedfastly in prayer, with **the** women **and children,** and Mary the mother of Jesus, and [with] his brethren.

15 And in these days Peter stood up in the midst of the **disciples,** and said (**for** there was a multitude of persons
16 together about a hundred and twenty), **Men and** brethren, it was needful that **this** scripture should be fulfilled, which the Holy Spirit spake before by the mouth of David concerning Judas, who was guide to them that took Jesus.
17 For he was numbered among us, and received his portion
18 in this ministry. Now this man obtained a field with the reward of his iniquity; and falling headlong he burst
19 asunder in the midst, and all his bowels gushed out. And it became known to all the dwellers at Jerusalem; insomuch that in their language that field was called Akeldamach, that is, The field of blood.

20 For it is written in the book of Psalms,
>> Let his habitation be made desolate,
>> And let no man dwell therein:
>> And his overseership let another take.

21 Of the men therefore which have companied with us all the time that the Lord Jesus **Christ** went in and went out
22 among us, beginning from the baptism of John, unto the day that he was received up from us, of these must one
23 become a witness with us of his resurrection. And **he** put forward two, Joseph called **Barnabas,** who was surnamed
24 Justus, and Matthias. And they prayed, and said, Thou,

Lord, which knowest the hearts of all men, shew of these
25 two the one whom thou hast chosen, to take the place in
this ministry and apostleship, from which Judas fell away,
26 that he might go to his own place. And they gave lots for
them; and the lot fell upon Matthias; and he was numbered
with the **twelve** apostles.

CHAPTER II

1 AND **it came to pass in those days** of the fulfilment of
the day of the Pentecost, when they were all [together] in
2 one place, and, **behold,** suddenly there came from heaven
a sound as of a rushing mighty wind, and it filled all the
3 house where they were sitting. And there appeared unto
them tongues parting asunder, like as of fire: and **they** sat
4 upon each one of them. And they were all filled with the
Holy Spirit, and began to speak with other tongues, as the
Spirit gave them utterance.

5 [Now] there were dwelling in Jerusalem Jews, devout
6 men, from every nation under heaven. And when this
sound took place, the multitude came together, and were
confounded; **and** each one heard them speaking in their
7 own **tongues.** And they were [all] amazed and marvelled,
saying to one another, Behold are not all these which
8 speak Galilæans? And how hear we each one our own
9 language wherein we were born? Parthians and Medes and
Elamites, and dwellers in Mesopotamia, Judæa and Cappa-
10 docia, in Pontus and Asia, in Phrygia and Pamphylia, in
Egypt and the parts of Libya about Cyrene, and sojourners
11 from Rome, both Jews and proselytes, Cretans and
Arabians, we do hear them speaking in our tongues the
12 mighty works of God. And they were all amazed, and
were perplexed, one with another, **about what had taken**
13 **place, and** saying What meaneth this? but others mock-
ing said, They are filled with **new wine.**

14 But **then** Peter, standing up with the **ten apostles,** lifted up his voice **first,** and **said,** Ye men of Judæa, and all ye that dwell at Jerusalem, be this known unto **us,**
15 [and] give ear unto my words. For these are not drunken, as ye suppose; seeing it is but the third hour of the day:
16 but this is that which hath been spoken by the prophet [Joel]:

17   [And] it shall be in the last days, saith the Lord,
    I will pour forth of my Spirit upon all flesh;
    And **their** sons and **their** daughters shall prophesy,
    And **the** young men shall see visions,
    And **the** old men shall dream dreams;
18   [yea] and on my servants and on my hand maidens [in those days]
    I will pour out of my Spirit;
    [And they shall prophesy].
19   And I will shew wonders in the heaven above,
    and signs on the earth beneath,
    [blood, and fire, and vapour of smoke].
20   the sun shall be turned into darkness,
    and the moon into blood,
    before the day of the Lord come,
    that great [and notable day].
21   And it shall be, that whosoever shall call on the name of the Lord shall be saved.

22 Ye men of Israel, hear these words, Jesus of Nazareth, a man approved of God unto **us** by mighty works and wonders and signs, which God did by him in the midst of
23 you, even as ye yourselves know; him, being delivered up by the determinate counsel and fore-knowledge of God, ye **took, and** by the hand of lawless men did crucify and slay;
24 whom God raised up, having loosed the pains of **Hades,** because it was not possible that he should be holden of it.
25 For David saith concerning him,

> I beheld **my** Lord always before my face;
> For he is on my right hand, that I should not be moved;
26 Therefore my heart was glad, and my tongue rejoiced;
> Moreover my flesh also shall dwell in hope:
27 Because thou wilt not leave my soul in Hades,
> Neither wilt thou give thy Holy One to see corruption.
28 Thou madest known unto me the ways of life;
> Thou shalt make me full of gladness with thy countenance.

29 **Men and** brethren, I may say unto you freely of the patri-
arch David, that he both died and was buried, and his tomb
30 is with us unto this day. Being therefore a prophet, and
knowing that God had sworn with an oath to him, that of
the fruit of **his heart according to the flesh he would**
31 **raise up the Christ,** and set him upon his throne*: [he
foreseeing this spake] of the resurrection of the Christ, that
neither was he left in Hades, nor did his flesh see corruption.
32 This Jesus **therefore** did God raise up, whereof we all are
33 witnesses. Being therefore by the right hand of God
exalted, and having received of the Father the promise of
the Holy Spirit, he hath poured forth **upon you** this, which
34 ye **both** see and hear. For David ascended not into the
heavens; for he **said** himself

> The Lord said unto my Lord,
> Sit thou on my right hand,
35 Till I make thine enemies
> The footstool of thy feet.

36 Let all the house of Israel know assuredly that God hath
made [him] both Lord and Christ, this Jesus whom ye
crucified.

37 Then all **who had come together,** when they heard
this, were pricked in their heart, and **some of them** said
to Peter and the [rest of the] apostles, **Men and** brethren,

---

* A line of MS. in D accidentally omitted in both versions.

38 what **therefore** shall we do? **Shew us.** And Peter saith unto them, Repent ye, and be baptized every one of you in the name of the **Lord** Jesus Christ unto the remission of [your] sins; and ye shall receive the gift of the Holy
39 Spirit. For to **us** is the promise, and to **our** children, and to all that are afar off, even as many as the Lord our God
40 shall call unto him. And with many other words he testified, and exhorted them, saying, Save yourselves from this
41 crooked generation. They then that **believed** his word were baptized; and there were added [unto them] in that
42 day about three thousand souls. And they continued stedfastly in the apostles' teaching **in Jerusalem,** and the fellowship, in the breaking of the bread, and the prayers*.
43 And fear came upon every soul: and many wonders and
44 signs were done by the Apostles. And all that believed
45 were together, and had all things common; and **as many as had** possessions or goods sold them, and parted them
46 **day by day** to all those who had need. And **all** continued stedfastly [with one accord], in the temple, and in their homes together breaking bread they did take their food
47 with gladness and singleness of heart, praising God, and having favour with all the **world.** And the Lord added [to them] those that were being saved day by day **together in the Church.**

Chapter III

1 **Now in those days** Peter and John were going up into the temple **in the evening** at the ninth hour, that of prayer.
2 And, **behold,** a certain man, that was lame from his mother's womb was being carried, whom they laid daily at the door of the temple which is called Beautiful, to ask
3 alms of them that were entering into the temple. **He fixing steadily his eyes, and** seeing Peter and John about to

* d, in the fellowship of the breaking of the bread.

4 go into the temple, asked alms **from them.** And Peter,
5 looking on him, with John, said, Look **steadily** on us. And
he **looked steadily on them,** expecting to receive some-
6 thing from them. But Peter said, Silver and gold have I
none; but what I have, that give I thee. In the name of
7 Jesus Christ of Nazareth, walk. And he took him by the
right hand, and raised him up. And immediately **he stood;**
8 **and** his feet and ankle-bones received strength. And leaping up, he stood, and walked **rejoicing,** and entered with
them into the temple [walking, and leaping, and] praising
9 God: And all the people saw him walking and praising
10 God. And they took knowledge of him, that it was he which
sat for alms at the Beautiful Gate of the temple; and they
were filled with wonder and amazement at that which had
happened unto him.
11 And **as Peter and John went out,** he **went out with
them, and** held them: and [all the people ran together
unto them and] were **standing** astonished in the porch
12 that is called Solomon's, greatly wondering. But Peter
answering said unto them: Ye men of Israel, why marvel
ye at this? or why fasten ye your eyes on us, as though by
our own power or godliness we had done **this thing** that he
13 should walk? The God of Abraham and **the God** of Isaac,
and **the God** of Jacob, the God of our fathers hath glorified
his servant Jesus **Christ,** whom ye delivered up **to judgment,** and denied him before the face of Pilate, when he
14 had **judged and wished** to release him. But ye **oppressed**
the Holy and Righteous One, and asked for a murderer to
15 be granted unto you. And ye killed the Prince of life;
whom God raised from the dead; whereof we are witnesses.
16 And by faith in his name **ye behold this man and know
that his name made him strong,** and the faith which is
by him hath given him this perfect soundness in the presence
17 of you all. And now, **men and** brethren, **we** know that ye

did **a wicked thing** in ignorance, as did also your rulers.
18 But the things which God foreshewed by the mouth of all the prophets, that his Christ should suffer, he hath thus
19 fulfilled. Repent ye therefore, and turn again, that your sins may be blotted out, that so there may come seasons
20 of refreshing from the face of the Lord; and that he may send the Christ who hath been appointed for you, even
21 Jesus, whom the heaven must receive until the times of restoration of all things, whereof God spake by the mouth of his holy prophets [which have been since the world
22 began.] Moses indeed said **unto our fathers,** A prophet shall the Lord your God raise up unto you of our brethren; to him **like unto myself** shall ye hearken in all things
23 whatsoever he shall speak unto you. And it shall be, that every soul, which shall not hearken to that prophet, shall
24 be utterly destroyed from among the people. Yea, and all the prophets, from Samuel and them that followed after, as many as have spoken, they also told of these days.
25 Ye are the sons of the prophets, and of the covenant which God made with your fathers, saying unto Abraham, And in thy seed shall all the families of the earth be blessed.
26 Unto you first, God having raised up his Servant, sent him to bless you, in turning away every one of you from your iniquities.

Chapter IV

1 AND as they spake **these words** unto the people, the priests and [the captain of the temple] and the Sadducees
2 came upon them, being sore troubled because they taught the people, and proclaimed **Jesus in the resurrection of**
3 **the dead.** And they laid hands on them, and put them in
4 ward unto the morrow: for it was now eventide. But many of them that heard the word believed; and the number **also** of the men came to be about five thousand.

5 And it came to pass on the **day of the** morrow, that **the** rulers and elders and Scribes were gathered together in
6 Jerusalem; and Annas the high-priest, and Caiaphas, and **Jonathas** and Alexander, and as many as were of the
7 kindred of the high-priest. And when they had set them in the midst, they inquired, By what power, or in what
8 name, have ye done this? Then Peter, filled with the Holy Spirit, said unto them, Ye rulers of the people, and elders
9 of **Israel,** if we this day are examined **by you** concerning a good deed done to an impotent man, by what means this
10 man is made whole; be it known unto you all, and to all the people of Israel, that in the name of Jesus Christ of Nazareth, whom ye crucified, whom God raised from the dead, in him doth this man stand here before you whole.
11 He is the stone which was set at nought of you the builders,
12 which was made the head of the corner. And in none other is there [salvation], for there is none other name under heaven given **to** men, wherein we must be saved.
13 Now when they beheld the boldness of Peter and John, and had perceived that they were unlearned [and ignorant] men, they marvelled; but they took knowledge of them,
14 that they had been with Jesus. [And] seeing the man that was healed standing with them, they could **do or** say
15 nothing against it. [But] when they had commanded that they **should be led** out of the Council, they conferred
16 among themselves, saying, What shall we do to these men? for that indeed a notable sign hath been wrought through them is **more than** manifest to all that dwell in Jerusalem,
17 and we cannot deny it. [But] that it spread no further among the people, let us threaten them, that they speak
18 henceforth to no man in this name. And **when they had agreed to this decision** they called them, and charged them
19 not to speak [at all] nor teach in the name of Jesus. But Peter and John answered and said unto them, Whether it

be right in the sight of God to hearken unto you rather than
20 unto God, judge ye: for we cannot* [but] speak the things
21 which we saw and heard. And they, when they had further
threatened them, let them go, finding nothing how they might
punish them, because of the people; for all men glorified God
22 for that which was done. For the man was more than forty
years old, on whom this sign of healing was wrought.

23 And being let go, they came to their own company, and
reported all that the chief priests and the elders had said
24 unto them. And they, when they heard it, **and recognised
the working of God,** lifted up their voice to God with
one accord, and said, O Lord, thou **the God** that didst
make the heaven and the earth and the sea, and all that in
25 them is: who by the Holy Spirit, by the mouth of [our
father] David thy servant didst say,

    Why did the Gentiles rage,
    And the peoples imagine vain things?
26   The kings of the earth set themselves in array,
    And the rulers were gathered together,
    Against the Lord, and against his Anointed:

27 For of a truth in this city, against thy holy Servant Jesus,
whom thou didst anoint, both Herod and Pontius Pilate
were gathered together with the Gentiles and the peoples
28 of Israel, to do whatsoever thy hand and thy counsel fore-
29 ordained to come to pass. And now, Lord, look upon their
threatenings: and grant unto thy servants to speak thy
30 word with all boldness, while thou stretchest forth thy
hand to heal, and that signs and wonders may be done
31 through the name of thy holy Servant Jesus. And when
they had prayed, the place was shaken wherein they were
gathered together: and they were all filled with the Holy
Spirit, and they spake the word of God with boldness, **to
every man who wished to believe.**

    * D and d, accidentally omit the second *not*.

32 And the multitude of them that believed were of one heart and soul, **and there was no distinction at all among them:** and not one of them said that aught of the things which he possessed was his own; but they had all
33 things common. And with great power gave the apostles their witness of the resurrection of the Lord Jesus **Christ;** and great grace was upon them all. For neither was there
34 among them any that lacked; for as many as were possessed of lands or houses sold them, and brought the prices of the
35 things that were sold, and laid them at the apostles' feet: and distribution was made unto each **one** according as any one had need.
36 And Joseph, who by the apostles was surnamed Barnabas, (which is, being interpreted, Son of Exhortation), a **Cyprian**
37 **Levite** by race, having a field sold it, and brought the money, and laid it at the apostles' feet.

CHAPTER V

1 BUT a certain man named Ananias, with Sapphira his wife,
2 sold a possession and kept back part of the price, his wife also being privy to it, and brought a certain part, and laid
3 it at the apostles' feet. But Peter said **to** Ananias, Why hath Satan filled thy heart to lie to the Holy Spirit, to
4 keep back part of the price of the land? Whiles it remained, did it not remain thine own? and after it was sold was it not in thy power? How is it that thou hast conceived in thy heart **to do** this **wicked** thing? thou hast not lied unto
5 men but unto God. And when he heard these words Ananias **immediately** fell down and gave up the ghost,
6 and great fear came upon all that heard it. And the young men arose and wrapped him round, and they carried him out and buried him.
7 And it was about the space of three hours after when
8 his wife, not knowing what was done, came in. And Peter

said to her **I will further ask you if verily** ye sold the
9 land for so much. She **then** said, Yea, for so much. But
Peter (said) unto her, How is it that ye have agreed together to tempt the Spirit of the Lord? Behold, the feet
of them which have buried thy husband are at the door,
10 and they shall carry thee out. And she fell down immediately at his feet, and gave up the ghost. And the young
men came in, and found her dead; and **having wrapped
her round** they carried her out, and buried her by her
11 husband. And great fear fell upon the whole church, and
upon all that heard these things.
12 And by the hands of the apostles were many signs and
wonders wrought among the people; and they were all with
13 one accord **in the temple** in Solomon's porch. But of the
rest* durst no one join himself to them; howbeit the people
14 magnified them. And were the more added to them, believing on the Lord, multitudes both of men and women:
15 insomuch that they [even] carried out **their** sick into the
streets, and laid them on beds and couches, that, as Peter
came by, at the least his shadow might overshadow some
one of them. **For they were set free from every sickness**
16 **which each one of them had.** And there came [also]
together into Jerusalem a multitude from the cities round
about, bringing sick folk, and them that were vexed with
unclean spirits: and all were **cured**†.
17 But the high priest rose up, and all they that were with
him which is the sect of the Sadducees, and they were
18 filled with jealousy; and laid hands on the apostles, and
put them in public ward: **and each one of them went to**
19 **his own home. Then** by night an angel of the Lord opened

* "The rest" is perplexing. Hilgenfeld conjectures "of the Levites,"
the words in Greek having some resemblance.

† The word in the *a* text, translated in A.V. and R.V. healed, is
θεραπεύειν, which means "treated" or "relieved": in the β text it
is ἰᾶσθαι, which means "cured." See Introduction, Section 23.

the doors of the prison, and brought them out, and said,
20 Go and stand and speak in the temple to the people all the
21 words of this Life. And when they heard this, they entered
into the temple about day break, and taught. But the
high priest came, and they that were with him, **having been
roused early,** and called the council together, and all the
senate of the children of Israel, and sent to the prison to
22 have them brought. But the officers having come **and
opened the prison** found them not within; and they
23 returned, and told, saying, The prison-house we found shut
in all safety, and the keepers standing at the doors; but
24 when we had opened we found no man within. Now when
the captain of the temple and the chief priests heard these
words, they were much perplexed concerning them where-
25 unto this would grow. And there came one and told them,
Behold the men whom ye put in the prison are in the
26 temple, standing and teaching the people. Then went the
captain with the officers, and brought them [not] with
violence: for they feared the people, lest they should be
27 stoned. And when they had brought them they set them
before the Council. And the [high] priest asked them,
28 saying, **Did we not** straitly charge you not to teach in this
name? And, behold, ye have filled Jerusalem with your
teaching, and wish to bring that man's blood upon us.
29 But Peter [and the apostles answered and] said **to them,**
30 We must obey God rather than men. The God of our fathers
raised up Jesus, whom ye slew, hanging him on a tree.
31 Him did God exalt **for his glory*** [with his right hand],
to be a Prince and a Saviour, to give repentance to Israel,
32 and remission of sins **in him.** And we are witnesses of **all**
these things; and so is the Holy Spirit, whom God hath
given to them that obey him.

* The Greek words "for his glory" closely resemble those for
"with his right hand."

33 But they, when they heard this, were cut to the heart,
34 and were minded to slay them. But there stood up one of the council, a Pharisee, named Gamaliel, a doctor of the law, had in honour of all the people, and commanded to
35 put **the apostles** forth a little while. And he said **to the rulers and those of the council,** Ye men of Israel, take heed to yourselves as touching these men, what ye are
36 about to do. For before these days rose up Theudas, giving himself out to be somebody **great**: to whom a number of men, about four hundred, joined themselves; who was slain **by himself,** and all as many as obeyed him, and came to
37 nought. After this man rose up Judas of Galilee, in the days of the enrolment, and drew away **much** people after him: he also perished, and all, as many as obeyed him,
38 were scattered abroad. And now, **brethren;** I say unto you, Refrain from these men, and let them alone, **not defiling your hands;** for if this counsel or this work be of
39 men, it will be overthrown; but if it is of God, ye will not be able to hinder them: **neither you nor kings nor tyrants: keep away therefore from these men,** lest
40 haply ye be found fighting against God. And to him they agreed: and when they had called the apostles unto them, they beat them, and charged them not to speak in
41 the name of Jesus, and let them go. The **apostles** therefore departed from the presence of the Council, rejoicing that they were counted worthy to suffer dishonour for the Name.
42 And every day, in the temple and at home they ceased not to teach and preach the **Lord** Jesus as the Christ.

CHAPTER VI

1 Now in these days, when the number of the disciples was multiplying, there arose a murmuring of the Hellenists against the Hebrews, because their widows were neglected in the daily ministration, **in the ministration of the**

2 **Hebrews.** [And] the twelve called the multitude of the disciples unto them, and said, It is not pleasing to us that we should leave the word of God, and minister to tables.
3 **What is it then,** brethren? Look ye out [therefore] from among you seven men of good report, full of the Spirit and of wisdom, whom we will appoint over this business:
4 but we will continue stedfastly in prayer, and in the ministry
5 of the word. And **this** saying pleased the whole multitude **of the disciples;** and they chose Stephen, a man full of faith and of the Holy Spirit, and Philip, and Prochorus, and **Nicor,** and Timon, and Parmenas, and Nicolas a
6 proselyte of Antioch. **These** were set before the apostles; and when they had prayed, they laid their hands on them.
7 And the word of the Lord increased; and the number of the disciples multiplied in Jerusalem exceedingly; and a great company of the priests were obedient to the faith.
8 And Stephen, full of grace and power, wrought great wonders and signs among the people, **through the name**
9 **of the Lord Jesus Christ.** But there arose certain of them that were of the Synagogue called the Synagogue of the Libertines, and of the Cyrenians, and of the Alexandrians, and of them of Cilicia [and Asia] disputing with
10 Stephen. And they were not able to withstand the wisdom **that was in him,** and the **Holy** Spirit with which he spake, **because they were confuted by him with all**
11 **boldness. Being unable therefore to face the truth** then they suborned men which said, We have heard him speak blasphemous words against Moses, and against God.
12 And they stirred up the people, and the elders, and the scribes, and came upon him, and seized him, and brought
13 him into the Council; and set up false witnesses **against him,** which said, This man ceaseth not to speak words
14 against **the** holy place, and the law: for we have heard him say that this Jesus of Nazareth shall destroy this place,

and shall change the customs which Moses delivered unto
15 us. And all that sat in the council, fastening their eyes on
him, saw his face as it had been the face of an angel **standing in the midst of them***.

Chapter VII

1 And the high priest said **to Stephen, Is this thing** so?
2 And he said **Men,** brethren and fathers, hearken. The God
of glory appeared to our father Abraham, when he was in
3 Mesopotamia, before he dwelt in Haran, and said unto
him, Get thee out of thy land, and from thy kindred, and
4 come into the land which I shall shew thee. Then came
Abraham out of the land of the Chaldeans, and dwelt in
Haran; and **there he was** after the death of his father.
And (God) removed him into this land, wherein ye now
5 dwell, **and our fathers who were before us.** And he
gave him none inheritance in it, no, not so much as to set
his foot on: **but** he promised that he would give it him in
possession, and his seed after him, when as yet he had no
6 child. And God spake on this wise **to him,** that his seed
should sojourn in a strange land, and that they should
bring them into bondage, and entreat them evil, four
7 hundred years. And the nation to which they shall be in
bondage will I judge, said God, and after that shall they
8 come forth, and serve me in this place. And he gave him
the covenant of circumcision. And so he begat Isaac, and
circumcised him the eighth day; and Isaac begat Jacob,
9 and Jacob the twelve patriarchs. And the patriarchs,
moved with jealousy against Joseph, sold him into Egypt;
10 and God was with him, and delivered him out of all his
afflictions, and gave him favour and wisdom before Pharaoh,
King of Egypt; and he made him governor over Egypt and

* It is possible that these words have been misplaced, and refer
to the high priest in the verse that follows. Rendel Harris, pp. 71–75.

11 all his house. Now there came a famine over all Egypt and
Canaan, and great affliction; and our fathers found no
12 sustenance. When **therefore** Jacob heard that there was
corn in Egypt, he sent forth our fathers the first time.
13 And at the second time Joseph was made known to his
brethren, and Joseph's race became manifest unto Pharaoh.
14 And Joseph sent, and called to him Jacob his father and
15 all his kindred, three score and fifteen souls. And Jacob
went down into Egypt; and he died, himself, and our fathers.
16 And they were carried over unto Shechem, and laid in the
tomb that Abraham bought for a price in silver of the sons
17 of Emmor **of** Shechem. But as the time of the promise
drew nigh, which God **promised** unto Abraham, the
18 people grew and multiplied in Egypt, till there arose
19 another king [over Egypt] which knew not Joseph. The
same dealt subtilly with our race, and evil entreated **the**
fathers, that they should cast out their babes to the end
they might not live.
20 At which season Moses was born, and was exceeding fair;
and he was nourished three months in his father's house.
21 And when he was cast out **by the riverside,** Pharaoh's
22 daughter took him up and nourished him for her own son.
And Moses was instructed in all the wisdom of the Egyptians,
23 and he was mighty in his words and works. But when he
was full forty years old it came into his heart to visit his
24 brethren the children of Israel. And seeing one **of his race**
suffering wrong, he defended him, and avenged him that
was oppressed, smiting the Egyptian, **and he hid him in**
25 **the sand;** and he supposed that his brethren understood
how that God by his hand was giving them deliverance;
26 but they understood not. And **then** on the day following
he appeared unto them as they strove, **and saw them
doing injustice,** and would have set them at one again,
saying, **What are ye doing,** men and brethren? why do

27 ye wrong one to another? But he that did his neighbour wrong thrust him away saying, Who made thee a ruler and
28 a judge over us? Wouldest thou kill me as thou killedst
29 the Egyptian yesterday? **Thus also** Moses fled at this saying, and became a sojourner in the land of Midian, where he begat two sons.
30 And **after these things,** when forty years were fulfilled, an angel **of the Lord** appeared to him in the wilderness
31 of Mount Sinai, in a flame of fire in a bush. And when Moses saw it, he wondered at the sight: and as he drew
32 near to behold, the Lord **spake to him** saying, I am the God of thy fathers, the God of Abraham, and **the God** of Isaac, and **the God** of Jacob. And Moses trembled, and
33 durst not behold. And **a voice** came to him, Loose the shoes from thy feet: for the place whereon thou standest
34 is holy ground. I have surely seen the affliction of my people which is in Egypt, and have heard their groaning, and I am come down to deliver them: and now come, I will send thee into Egypt.
35 This Moses whom they refused, saying, Who made thee a ruler and a judge **over us**, him hath God sent to be both a ruler and a redeemer with the hand of the angel which
36 appeared to him in the bush. This man led them forth, having wrought wonders and signs in Egypt, and in the
37 Red Sea, and in the wilderness forty years. This is [that] Moses, which said unto the children of Israel, A prophet shall God raise up unto you from among your brethren, as
38 he raised up me: **hear him.** This is he that was in the church in the wilderness with the angel which spake to him in the mount Sinai, and **of** our fathers; who received living
39 oracles to give unto us: **because** our fathers would not be obedient, but thrust him from them, and turned back in
40 their hearts unto Egypt, saying unto Aaron, Make us gods which shall go before us: for **as** for this Moses, which led

us forth out of the land of Egypt, we wot not what is become
41 of him. And they made a calf in those days, and brought
a sacrifice unto the idol, and rejoiced in the works of their
42 hands. But God turned, and gave them up to serve the
host of heaven; as it is written in the book of the prophets,

> Did ye offer unto me slain beasts and sacrifices,
> forty years in the wilderness, O house of Israel?

43 And ye took up the tabernacle of Moloch,
and the star of the god Remphan,
the figures which ye made to worship them;
and I will carry you away into **the parts** of Babylon.

44 The tabernacle of the testimony was with our fathers in the wilderness, even as he appointed who spake unto Moses that he should make it according to the figure that he had
45 seen. Which also our fathers, in their turn, brought in with Joshua when they entered on the possession of the nations, which God thrust out before the face of our fathers, unto
46 the days of David; who found favour in the sight of God,
47 and asked to find a habitation for the **house** of Jacob. But
48 Solomon built him a house. Howbeit the Most High dwelleth not in houses made with hands, as saith the prophet,

49 The heaven is my throne,
and the earth the footstool of my feet.
What manner of house will ye build me? saith the Lord:
or of **what sort** is the place of my rest?
50 Did not my hand make all these things?

51 Ye stiffnecked and uncircumcised in heart and ears, ye do always resist the Holy Spirit: as your fathers did, so do ye.
52 Which of the prophets did not they persecute? and they killed them which shewed before of the coming of the Righteous One; of whom ye have now become betrayers
53 and murderers; ye who received the law as it was ordained by angels, and kept it not.

54 Now when they heard these things, they were cut to the
55 heart, and they gnashed on him with their teeth. But he, being full of the Holy Spirit, looked up stedfastly into heaven, and saw the glory of God, and Jesus **the Lord,**
56 standing on the right hand of God: and said, Behold I see the heavens opened, and the Son of Man standing on the
57 right hand of God. But they cried out with a loud voice, and stopped their ears, and rushed upon him with one
58 accord; and they cast him out of the city, and stoned him; and the witnesses laid down their garments at the feet of
59 a **certain** young man named Saul. And they stoned Stephen calling upon [the Lord] and saying, Lord Jesus, receive my
60 spirit. And he kneeled down, and cried with a loud voice, **saying,** Lord, lay not this sin to their charge; and when he had said this, he fell asleep.

Chapter VIII

1 And Saul was consenting unto his death.

And there arose on that day a great persecution **and affliction** against the church which was in Jerusalem; and they were all scattered abroad throughout the regions of Judæa and Samaria, except the apostles, **who remained**
2 **in Jerusalem.** And devout men buried Stephen, and made
3 great lamentation over him. But Saul laid waste the church, entering into every house, and haling men and women, committed them to prison.

4 They therefore that were scattered abroad went about
5 preaching the word. And Philip went down to the city of
6 Samaria, and proclaimed unto them the Christ. And, **when they heard,** all the multitudes gave heed unto the things which were spoken by Philip with one accord*, when they
7 heard and saw the signs which he did. For from many of those which had unclean spirits they came out crying with

* The Greek text is defective here.

a loud voice, and many that were palsied [and that were]
8 lame were healed*. And there was much joy in that city.
9 But there was a certain man, Simon by name, which beforetime in the city used sorcery, and amazed the people of Samaria, giving out that he himself was some great one;
10 to whom they all gave heed from the least to the greatest, saying, This man is the power of God which is called Great.
11 And they gave heed to him, because that of long time he
12 had amazed them with his sorceries. But when they believed Philip preaching good tidings concerning the kingdom of God and the name of Jesus Christ, they were
13 baptized, both men and women. And Simon also himself believed, and **was** baptized, and he continued with Philip; and beholding signs and great miracles wrought, he was
14 amazed. Now when the apostles which were at Jerusalem heard that Samaria had received the word of God, they
15 sent unto them Peter and John; who when they were come down, prayed for them, that they might receive the Holy
16 Spirit: for as yet he was fallen upon none of them: only they had been baptized into the name of the Lord Jesus
17 **Christ.** Then laid they their hands upon them, and they
18 received the Holy Spirit. Now when Simon saw that through the laying on of the apostles' hands the Holy
19 Spirit was given, he brought them money, **exhorting them** and saying, Give me also this power, that on whomsoever I **also** lay my hands, he may receive the Holy Spirit.
20 But Peter said unto him, Thy silver perish with thee, because thou hast thought to obtain the gift of God with
21 money. Thou hast neither part nor lot in this matter, for
22 thy heart is not right before God. Repent therefore from this thy wickedness, and pray the Lord if perhaps the
23 thought of thy heart shall be forgiven thee: for I see that thou art in the gall of bitterness and in the bond of iniquity.

* Treated medically or relieved.

24 And Simon answered and said **to them I beseech you** pray ye for me to **God** that none of these **evils of** which ye have spoken come upon me. **And he ceased not to shed many tears.**
25 They therefore, when they had testified and spoken the word of the Lord, returned to Jerusalem, and preached the gospel to many villages of the Samaritans.
26 But an angel of the Lord spake unto Philip saying, Arise, and go toward the south unto the way that goeth down
27 from Jerusalem unto Gaza: the same is desert. And he arose and went: and, behold, a man of Ethiopia, an eunuch of great authority under Candace, **a certain** queen of the Ethiopians, who had the charge of all her treasure, who
28 had come to Jerusalem for to worship: and he was returning and sitting in his chariot [and was] reading the prophet
29 Isaiah. And the Spirit said unto Philip...

> Here eight leaves of the Codex are wanting, including from viii. 29 to x. 14 in Greek, and viii. 20 to x. 4 in Latin.
> The Latin text, d, follows α from x. 4 to x. 14.

Chapter X. 14

14
15 ...anything that is common **or** unclean **and called** unto him again the second time, What God hath cleansed, make
16 not thou common. And this was done thrice: and [straight
17 way] the vessel was received up **again** into heaven. Now **when he came to himself** Peter doubted what this vision which he had seen should mean: and, behold the men that were sent **from** Cornelius, having made enquiry for Simon's
18 house, stood before the gate, and called and asked whether
19 Simon, which was surnamed Peter, was lodging there. And while Peter thought on the vision, the Spirit said unto him,
20 Behold [three] men seek thee. But arise, and get thee down,

and go with them nothing doubting; for I have sent them.
21 **Then** Peter went down to the men and said, Behold I am
he whom ye seek. **What do you wish?** or what is the
22 cause wherefore ye are come? And they said **to him,** A
certain Cornelius, a centurion, a righteous man, and one
that feareth God, and well reported of by all the nation of
the Jews, was warned by a holy angel to send for thee into
23 his house, and to hear words from thee. Then **Peter led**
them in and lodged them.
24 And on the morrow he arose and went forth with them,
and certain of the brethren from Joppa accompanied him.
And on the morrow **he** entered into Cæsarea. And Cornelius
was expecting them, and having called together his
kinsmen and his near friends he was waiting for them.
25 **And as Peter was drawing near to Cæsarea one of the
servants ran forward and announced that he was
come. And Cornelius sprang up and** met him, and fell
26 down at his feet, and worshipped him. But Peter raised
him up saying **What art thou doing?** I myself also am
27 a man **as thou also art.** And [as he talked with him] he
28 went in, and found many come together. And he said unto
them, Ye yourselves know **very well** how that it is an
unlawful thing for a man that is a Jew to join himself or
come unto one that is of another nation: and unto me hath
God shewed that I should not call any man common or
29 unclean. Wherefore also I came without gainsaying when
I was sent for **by you.** I ask therefore with what intent ye
30 sent for me. And Cornelius said, **From the third day**
until this hour **I was fasting,** and keeping the ninth hour
of prayer in my house, and behold, a man stood before me
31 in bright apparel, and saith, Cornelius, thy prayer is heard,
and thine alms are had in remembrance in the sight of God.
32 Send therefore to Joppa, and call unto thee Simon, who is
surnamed Peter; he lodgeth in the house of Simon a tanner

by the seaside. **He when he cometh shall speak unto**
33 **thee.** Forthwith therefore I sent to thee **exhorting thee
to come unto us;** and thou hast well done that thou hast
come **with speed.** Now therefore we all in **thy** sight are
wishing to hear **from thee** that which has been commanded
thee by **God.**

34 And Peter opened his mouth and said, Of a truth I per-
35 ceive that God is no respecter of persons; but in every
nation he that feareth him, and worketh righteousness, is
36 acceptable to him. **For** the word which he sent unto the
children of Israel, preaching good tidings of peace by Jesus
37 Christ, (he is Lord of all), ye know that [saying] which
took place throughout all Judæa; **for** beginning from
Galilee, after the baptism which John preached, even Jesus
38 of Nazareth, whom God anointed with the Holy Spirit and
with power. He went about doing good, and healing all
that were oppressed of the devil; for God was with him.
39 And we are **his** witnesses of [all] the things which he did both
in the country of the Jews, and in Jerusalem; whom also
40 they slew, hanging him on a tree. Him God raised up **after**
41 the third day, and gave him to be made manifest, not to
all the people, but unto witnesses that were chosen before
of God, even to us, who did eat and drink with him, **and
companied with him,** after he rose from the dead **for**
42 **forty days.** And he charged us to preach unto the people,
and to testify that this is he which is ordained of God to
43 be the Judge of quick and dead. To him bear all the prophets
witness, that through his name every one that believeth
on him shall receive remission of sins.

44 While Peter yet spake these words, the Holy Spirit fell
45 on all them that heard the word. And they of the circumcision which believed were amazed, as many as came with
Peter, because that on the Gentiles also was poured out the
46 gift of the Holy Spirit. For they heard them speak with

TRANSLATED FROM THE CODEX BEZÆ

47 uncertain* tongues and magnify God. And Peter said, Can any man forbid the water, that these should not be baptized,
48 which have received the Holy Spirit as well as we? Then he commanded them to be baptized in the name of **the Lord** Jesus Christ. Then they besought him to remain with them certain days.

CHAPTER XI

1 Now it was heard by the apostles and the brethren that were in Judæa that the Gentiles also had received the word
2 of God. Peter **therefore for a considerable time wished to journey to Jerusalem; and he called to him the brethren, and stablished them; making a long speech, and teaching them throughout the villages: he also went to meet them, and he reported to them the grace of** God. But **the brethren** that were of the circumcision
3 contended with him, saying, Thou wentest in to men un-
4 circumcised, and didst eat with them. But Peter began, and expounded the matter unto them in order, saying,
5 I was in the city of Joppa praying; and in a trance I saw a vision, a certain vessel descending, as it were a great sheet let down from heaven by four corners, and it came
6 even unto me. Upon the which when I had fastened mine eyes, I considered, and saw [the] fourfooted beasts of the earth, and the wild beasts, and creeping things, and fowls
7 of the heaven. And I heard [also] a voice saying unto me,
8 Rise, Peter, kill and eat. But I said, Not so, Lord; for nothing common or unclean hath ever entered into my
9 mouth. But **there was** a voice **to me** [the second time] out of heaven, What God hath cleansed, make not thou com-
10 mon. And this was done thrice; and all were drawn up
11 again into heaven. And behold, forthwith three men stood before the house in which we were, having been sent from

* The Greek is wanting; the Latin reads *prævaricatis linguis*.

12 Cæsarea unto me. And the Spirit bade me go with them [making no distinction]. And these six brethren also accompanied me; and we entered into the man's house;
13 and he told us how he had seen an angel standing in his house, and saying **to him,** Send to Joppa and fetch Simon,
14 whose surname is Peter, who shall speak unto thee words whereby thou shalt be saved, thou and all thy house.
15 And as I began to speak **to them,** the Holy Spirit fell on
16 them, even as on us at the beginning. And I remembered the word of the Lord, how that he said, John indeed baptized with water; but ye shall be baptized with the Holy
17 Spirit. If then [God] gave unto them the like gift as he did also unto us, when we believed on the Lord Jesus Christ, who was I that I could withstand God? **that I should not give them the Holy Spirit when they believed on him.**
18 And when they heard these things, they held their peace; and glorified God, saying, Then to the Gentiles also hath God given repentance unto life.
19 They therefore that were scattered abroad upon the tribulation that arose from Stephen travelled as far as Phœnicia and Cyprus and Antioch, speaking the word to
20 none save only to Jews. But there were some of them, men of Cyprus and Cyrene, who, when they were come to Antioch spake unto the Greeks [also], preaching the Lord
21 Jesus **Christ.** And the hand of the Lord was with them: and a great number that believed turned unto the Lord.
22 And the report concerning them came to the ears of the Church which was in Jerusalem: and they sent forth
23 Barnabas **that he should go** as far as Antioch; who **also,** when he had come, and had seen the grace of God, was glad; and exhorted them all, that with purpose of heart
24 they would cleave unto the Lord; for he was a good man, and full of the Holy Spirit and of faith: and much people was added unto the Lord.

25 And **having heard that Saul was at Tarsus,** he went out to seek him; and when he met him he **exhorted him** to come to Antioch.
26 And they, **when they had come,** for a whole year were gathered together (in the church, and taught)* much people, and the disciples were called Christians **then** first in Antioch.
27 Now in these days there came down prophets from
28 Jerusalem unto Antioch. **And there was much rejoicing; and when we were gathered together** one of them named Agabus stood up and spake, signifying by the Spirit that there should be a great famine over all the world;
29 which came to pass in the days of Claudius. And the disciples, every man according to his ability, determined to send for ministry unto the brethren who dwelt in Judæa;
30 which also they did, sending it to the elders by the hand of Barnabas and Saul.

Chapter XII

1 Now about that time Herod the king put forth his hands
2 to afflict certain of the Church **in Judæa.** And he killed
3 James the brother of John with the sword. And when he saw that **his laying hands upon the faithful** pleased the Jews, he proceeded to seize Peter also. And those were
4 the days of unleavened bread. And when he had taken him, he put him in prison, and delivered him to four quaternions of soldiers to guard him; intending after the
5 Passover to bring him forth to the people. Peter therefore was kept in the prison: but **much** prayer in earnestness **about him** was made by the church to God about him.
6 And when Herod was about to bring him forth, the same night Peter was sleeping between two soldiers, bound with

* A whole line omitted in error in both Greek and Latin texts.

two chains, and guards before the door were keeping the
7 prison. And behold an angel of the Lord stood by **Peter,**
and a light shined in the cell; and he **nudged** Peter on the
8 side, and awoke him, saying, Rise up quickly. And his
chains fell off from his hands. And the angel said unto
him, Gird thyself, and bind on thy sandals. And he did
so. And he saith unto him, Cast thy garment about thee
9 and follow me. And he went out and followed; and he wist
not that it was true which was done by the angel; **for** he
10 thought he saw a vision. And when they were past the
first and the second ward, they came unto the iron gate
that leadeth into the city, which opened to them of its own
accord, and they went out, **and went down the seven
steps,** and passed on through one street; and straightway
11 the angel departed from him. And when Peter was come
to himself, he said, Now I know of a truth, that the Lord
hath sent forth his angel and delivered me out of the hand
of Herod, and from all the expectation of the people of the
12 Jews. And when he had considered the thing, he came to
the house of Mary the mother of John, whose surname was
Mark; where many were gathered together and were pray-
13 ing. And when he knocked at the door of the gate, a maid
14 came to answer, named Rhoda. And when she knew Peter's
voice, she opened not the gate for joy, **and** ran in and told
15 that Peter stood before the gate. And they said unto her,
Thou art mad. But she confidently affirmed that it was
16 even so. And they said **Perchance** it is his angel. But
Peter continued knocking. And when they had opened and
17 saw him, they were astonished. But he, beckoning unto
them with the hand to hold their peace, **came in** and
declared unto them how that the Lord had brought him
forth out of the prison. And he said, Tell these things unto
James, and to the brethren. And he departed and went
18 to another place. Now as soon as it was day, there was a

[no small] stir among the soldiers, what was become of
19 Peter. And when Herod had sought for him, and found him not, he examined the guards, and commanded that they should be put to death. And he went down from Judæa to Cæsarea, and tarried there.
20 **For** he was highly displeased with them of Tyre and Sidon: **but** they with one accord **from both the cities** came **to the king,** and having persuaded Blastus the king's chamberlain, they asked for peace, because their country
21 was fed from the king's country. And upon a set day Herod arrayed himself in royal apparel, and sat on the throne, and made an oration unto them, **after being**
22 **reconciled with the Tyrians.** And the people shouted,
23 saying, The voice of a god, and not of a man. And immediately an angel of the Lord smote him, because he gave not God the glory. **And he came down from the throne, and while he was still living** he was eaten of worms, and **thus** gave up the ghost.
24 But the word of God grew and multiplied. And Barnabas
25 and Saul returned from Jerusalem when they had fulfilled their ministration, taking with them John, whose surname was Mark.

Chapter XIII

1 Now there were at Antioch, in the church that was there, prophets and teachers, **among whom were** Barnabas, and Symeon that was called Niger, and Lucius of Cyrene, and Manaen, the foster-brother of Herod the tetrarch, and
2 Saul. And as they ministered to the Lord, and fasted, the Holy Spirit said, Separate me Barnabas and Saul for the
3 work whereunto I have called them. Then when they had **all** fasted and prayed, and had laid their hands on them, [they sent them away.]*

* Probably a line here accidentally omitted.

4 So they, being sent forth by the Holy Spirit, went down
5 to Seleucia; and from thence they sailed to Cyprus. And
when they were at Salamis, they proclaimed the word **of
the Lord** in the Synagogues of the Jews; and they had
6 also John as their attendant. And when they had gone
through the whole island unto Paphos, they found a
certain sorcerer, a false prophet, a Jew, whose name was
7 Barjesus, which was with the proconsul, Sergius Paulus, a
man of understanding. The same called unto him Barnabas
8 and Saul, and sought to hear the word of God. But **Etimas**
the sorcerer (for so is his name by interpretation) withstood them, seeking to turn aside the proconsul from the
faith, **since he was hearing them with the greatest
9 pleasure.** But Saul who is also called Paul, filled with the
10 Holy Spirit, fastened his eyes on him, and said, O full of
all guile and all villany, thou son of the devil, thou enemy
of all righteousness, wilt thou not cease to pervert the ways
11 of the Lord **which are** right. And now, behold, the hand
of the Lord is upon thee, and thou shalt be blind, not seeing
the sun for a season. And immediately there fell on him a
mist and a darkness; and he went about seeking some to
12 lead him by the hand. And [then] the proconsul, when he
saw what was done **marvelled,** and believed **in God,**
being astonished at the teaching of the Lord.

13 Now Paul and his company set sail from Paphos, and
came to Perga of Pamphylia; but John departed from
14 them and returned to Jerusalem. But they, passing through
from Perga, came to Antioch of Pisidia; and they went into
15 the synagogue on the Sabbath day, and sat down. And
after the reading of the law and the prophets the rulers of
the synagogue sent unto them, saying, **Men and** brethren,
if ye have any word **of wisdom** of exhortation for the
16 people, say on. And Paul stood up and beckoning with
the hand said, Men of Israel, and ye that fear God, hearken.

17 The God of this people Israel chose our fathers and exalted*
the people when they sojourned in the land of Egypt, and
18 with a high arm led he them forth out of it, and for [about]
forty years† suffered he their manners in the wilderness.
19 And when he had destroyed seven nations in the land of
Canaan, he gave them the land **of the Philistines** for an
20 inheritance; and for about four hundred and fifty years he
21 gave them judges until Samuel the prophet. And afterwards they asked for a king: and God gave unto them Saul,
the son of Kish, a man of the tribe of Benjamin, for the
22 space of forty years. And when he had removed him, he
raised up David to be their king: to whom also he bare
witness, and said, I have found David the son of Jesse, a
23 man after my heart, who shall do all my will. Of this man's
seed **therefore** hath God according to promise **raised up**
24 unto Israel a Saviour, Jesus; when John had first preached
before his coming the baptism of repentance to all the
25 people of Israel. And as John was fulfilling his course, he
said, **Whom** suppose ye that I am? I am not he. But,
behold, there cometh one after me, the shoes of whose feet
26 I am not worthy to unloose. **Men and** brethren, children
of the stock of Abraham, and those among **us** who fear God,
27 to us is the word of this salvation sent forth. For they that
dwell at Jerusalem, and their rulers, [because they knew
him not,] nor understanding the **writings** of the prophets
which are read every Sabbath, fulfilled them by condemning
28 him. And though they found no cause of death in him,
after judging him they delivered him to Pilate that he
29 should be slain. And when they had fulfilled all things that
were written of him **they asked Pilate to crucify him.** And
when they had obtained this also, they took him down
30 from the tree, and laid him in a tomb; **whom** God raised

---

* D and d are both apparently corrupt in one line.
† The Latin text reads: "nourished them as a nurse."

31 from the dead. He was seen for many days of them that came up with him from Galilee to Jerusalem, who **till now**
32 are his witnesses unto the people. And we bring you good
33 tidings of the promise made unto the fathers, that God
34 hath fulfilled the same unto our children, in that he raised up the **Lord** Jesus **Christ. For thus** it is written in the **first** Psalm,

>Thou art my Son;
>this day have I begotten thee
>**Ask of me and I will give thee the heathen
>for thine inheritance,
>and the ends of the earth
>for thy possession.**

And when he raised him up from the dead, now no more to return to corruption, he hath spoken on this wise, I will give you the holy and sure blessings of David. And elsewhere he saith, Thou wilt not give thy Holy One to see corruption.
36 For David, after he had in his own generation served the counsel of God, fell on sleep, and was laid unto his fathers,
37 and saw corruption; but he whom God raised up saw no
38 corruption. Be it known unto you therefore, **men and** brethren, that through this man is proclaimed unto you remission of sins; and **repentance** from all things from
39 which ye could not be justified by the law of Moses. In
40 him **therefore** every one that believeth is justified **before God.** Beware therefore lest that come upon you which
41 is spoken in the prophets; Behold ye despisers and wonder and vanish away; for I work a work in your days. [a work] which ye shall in no wise believe if a man declare it unto you. **And they kept silence.**
42 And as they went out, they besought that these words
43 might be spoken to them the next Sabbath. Now when the synagogue broke up, many of the Jews and of the devout proselytes followed Paul and Barnabas; who speaking to

them urged them to continue in the grace of God. **And it came to pass that the word of God went throughout the whole city.**

44 And the next Sabbath almost the whole city was gathered together to hear **Paul telling about the Lord in many
45 words.** And when the Jews saw the multitudes, they were filled with jealousy, and contradicted the words which were
46 spoken by Paul, **contradicting and railing.** And Paul and Barnabas spake out boldly **unto them,** and said, It was **right** that the word of God should first be spoken to you: but seeing ye thrust it from you, and judge yourselves
47 unworthy of eternal life, lo, we turn to the Gentiles. For so hath the Lord commanded [us] saying, I have set thee for a light of the Gentiles, that thou shouldest be for salvation unto the uttermost part of the earth.
48 And as the Gentiles heard this, they were glad, and they **received** the word of God: and as many as were ordained
49 to eternal life believed. And the word of the Lord was
50 spread abroad throughout all the region. But the Jews urged on the devout women of honourable estate, and the chief men of the city, and stirred up a **great affliction and** persecution against Paul and Barnabas, and cast them out
51 of their borders. But they shook off the dust of their feet
52 against them, and went down to Iconium. And the disciples were filled with joy and with the Holy Spirit.

Chapter XIV

1 AND it came to pass in Iconium that **in the same way** he entered into the synagogue of the Jews, and so spake **to them** that a great multitude both of Jews and of Greeks
2 believed. But the rulers of the synagogue of the Jews [that were disobedient] **and the chief men of the synagogue raised up among them** a persecution against the just, and made the souls of the Gentiles evil affected against the

brethren. **But the Lord speedily gave them peace.**
3 Long time therefore they tarried there, speaking boldly in the Lord, which bare witness unto the word of his grace,
4 granting signs and wonders to be done by their hands. But the multitude of the city was divided, and part held with the Jews, and part with the apostles, **cleaving to them on
5 account of the word of God.** And when there was made an onset both of the Gentiles and of the Jews with their
6 rulers to entreat them shamefully and to stone them*, they became aware of it, and fled into the cities of Lycaonia, **to
7 Lystra and Derbe, and the whole** region round about. And there they preached the gospel. **And the whole multitude was moved at the teaching.**

Now Paul and Barnabas spent some time at Lystra.
8 And there sat a certain man impotent in his feet, [a cripple]
9 from his mother's womb, who never had walked. The same heard Paul speaking, **being in fear. And Paul,** fastening his eyes upon him, and seeing that he had faith to be saved,
10 said with a loud voice, **I say to thee in the name of the Lord Jesus Christ,** Stand upright on thy feet, **and walk.** And **straightway suddenly** he leaped up and
11 walked. And when the multitudes saw what Paul had done, they lifted up their voice, saying in the speech of Lycaonia, The gods are come down to us in the likeness of
12 men. And they called Barnabas, Zeus: and Paul, Hermes,
13 because he was the chief speaker. And the **priests** of Zeus, whose temple was before the city, brought **for them** oxen and garlands unto the gates, and would have done sacrifice
14 with the multitudes. But when [the apostles], Barnabas and Paul, heard of it, they rent their garments, and sprang forth among the multitude, crying out and **exclaiming,**
15 Sirs, why do ye these things? We also are men of like

* The Latin Version states that they did stone them at the second persecution.

passions with you, and bring you good tidings **of God,** that
ye should turn from these vain things unto the living God,
who made the heaven and the earth and the sea, and all
16 that in them is; who in the generations gone by suffered
17 **[all]** the nations to walk in their own ways. And yet he left
not himself without witness, in that he did good, and gave
you from heaven rains and fruitful seasons, filling your hearts
18 with food and gladness. And with those sayings scarce restrained they the multitudes from doing sacrifice unto them.
19 [But] **while they were spending some time there
and teaching** there came **certain** Jews from Iconium and
Antioch: and having persuaded the multitudes, they stoned
Paul, and dragged him out of the city, supposing that he
20 was dead. But as the disciples stood round about him, he
rose up, and entered into the city **of Lystra,** and on the
21 morrow he went forth with Barnabas to Derbe. And when
they had preached the gospel **to those in** the city, and had
made many disciples, they returned to Lystra and to Iconium
22 and to Antioch, confirming the souls of the disciples, **and**
exhorting them to continue in the faith, and that through
many tribulations we must enter into the kingdom of God.
23 And when they had appointed for them elders in every
church, and had prayed with fastings, they commended
24 them to the Lord on whom they had believed. And they
25 passed through Pisidia, and came to Pamphylia. And when
they had spoken the word in Perga, they went down to
26 Attalia, **preaching to them the good tidings.** And
thence they sailed to Antioch, from whence they had been
committed to the grace of God for the work which they had
27 fulfilled. And when they were come, and had gathered the
church together, they rehearsed all things that God had
done for them **with their souls,** and that he had opened
28 a door of faith unto the Gentiles. And they tarried no little
time with the disciples.

Chapter XV

1 AND certain men came down from Judæa and were teaching the brethren, saying, Except ye be circumcised **and
2 walk** after the custom of Moses, ye cannot be saved. And Paul and Barnabas had no small dissension and questioning with them, **for Paul spake strongly maintaining that they should remain so as when they believed; but those who had come from Jerusalem**, charged them, Paul and Barnabas and certain others [of them], to go up to Jerusalem unto the apostles and elders **that they might
3 be judged before them** about this question. They therefore, being brought on their way by the Church, passed through both Phœnicia and Samaria, declaring the conversion of the Gentiles; and they caused great joy to all
4 the brethren. And when they were come to Jerusalem, they were received **in great fashion** by the Church and the apostles and the elders, and they rehearsed all things
5 that God had done with them. But **those who had charged them to go up to the elders, being** certain of the sect of the Pharisees who believed, rose up saying, It is needful to circumcise them, and to charge them to keep the law of Moses.

6 And the apostles and elders were gathered together to
7 consider of this matter. And when there had been much questioning, Peter rose up **in the Spirit** and said unto them, **Men and** brethren, ye know how that a good while ago God made choice among **us** that by my mouth the Gentiles
8 should hear the word of the Gospel and believe. And God, which knoweth the heart, bare them witness, giving **upon**
9 them the Holy Spirit, even as he did unto us; and he made no distinction between us and them, cleansing their hearts
10 by faith. Now therefore why tempt ye God, that ye shall

put a yoke upon the neck of the disciples, which neither our
11 fathers nor we were able to bear? But we believe that we
shall be saved through the grace of the Lord Jesus **Christ,**
in like manner as they.
12 **And the elders agreed to what had been spoken by
Peter:** and all the multitude kept silence; and they
hearkened unto Barnabas and Paul rehearsing what signs
and wonders God had wrought among the Gentiles by them.
13 And after they had held their peace, James **rose up and**
14 said, **Men and** brethren, hearken unto me: Symeon hath
rehearsed how first God did visit the Gentiles, to take out
15 of them a people for his name. And to this agree the words
of the prophets, as it is written,
16 After these things I will return,
And I will build again the tabernacle of David which
is fallen;
And I will build again the ruins thereof,
And I will set it up;
17 That the residue of men may seek after the Lord,
And all the Gentiles upon whom my name is called
Saith the Lord who doeth these things.
18 Known **unto the Lord** from the beginning is his work.
19 Wherefore my judgment is that we trouble not them which
20 from among the Gentiles turn to God: but that we enjoin
on them to abstain from the pollutions of idols, and from
fornication, [and from what is strangled] and from blood:
and that whatsoever they would not should be done
21 **to them ye do not to others.** For Moses from generations
of old hath in every city them that preach him, being read
in the synagogues every Sabbath.
22 Then it seemed good to the apostles and elders, with the
whole church, to choose men out of their company and
send them to Antioch with Paul and Barnabas, Judas
called **Barabbas,** and Silas, chief men among the brethren,

23 And they wrote **a letter by their hands containing as follows.** The apostles and the elder brethren unto the brethren which are of the Gentiles in Antioch and Syria
24 and Cilicia, greeting: Forasmuch as we have heard that certain which went out from us have troubled you with words, subverting your souls; to whom we gave no com-
25 mandment; it seemed good unto us, having come to one accord, to choose out men, and send them to you with
26 **your** beloved Barnabas and Paul, men that have hazarded their lives for the name of our Lord Jesus Christ **in every**
27 **trial.** We have sent therefore Judas and Silas, who themselves also shall tell you the same things by word of mouth.
28 For it seemed good to the Holy Spirit and to us, to lay upon
29 you no greater burden than these necessary things; that ye abstain from idol sacrifices, and from blood, [and from things strangled], and from fornication **and whatsoever ye would not should be done to yourselves, not to do to another.** From which if ye keep yourselves ye do well, **being sustained by the Holy Spirit.** Fare ye well.
30 So they, when they were dismissed, **in a few days** came down to Antioch; and having gathered the multitude to-
31 gether, they delivered the epistle. And when they had read
32 it they rejoiced for the consolation. And Judas and Silas, being themselves also prophets, **full of the Holy Spirit** exhorted the brethren by [much] speech, and confirmed
33 them. And after they had spent some time there, they were dismissed in peace from the brethren unto those that
34 had sent them forth. **But it seemed good to Silas to**
35 **abide there, and Judas journeyed alone.** But Paul and Barnabas tarried in Antioch, teaching and preaching the word of the Lord, with many others also.
36 And after some days Paul said to Barnabas, Let us return now and visit the brethren in every city wherein we pro-
37 claimed the word of the Lord, and see how they fare. And

Barnabas was minded to take with them John [also] who was
38 called Mark. But Paul **was not willing: saying that one
who withdrew from them from Pamphylia,** and went
not with them to the work **for which they were sent,**
39 should not be with them. And there arose a sharp contention, so that they parted asunder one from the other. **Then**
40 Barnabas took Mark and sailed to Cyprus; but Paul chose
Silas, and went forth, being commended by the brethren to
41 the grace of the Lord. And he went through Syria and
Cilicia confirming the churches, **giving to them the
commands of the elders.**

Chapter XVI

1 **And having passed through these nations** he came
down to Derbe and Lystra, and, behold, a certain disciple
was there, named Timothy, the son of a Jewess which
2 believed; but his father was a Greek. The same was well
reported of by the brethren that were at Lystra and
3 Iconium. Him would Paul have to go forth with him; and
he took and circumcised him because of the Jews that were
in those parts: for they all knew that his father was a
4 Greek. And as they went through the cities **they preached
and delivered unto them, with all boldness, the Lord
Jesus Christ,** and **at the same time also** delivered
[them] the decrees [which had been ordained] of the
5 apostles and elders that were at Jerusalem. So the churches
were strengthened [in the faith], and increased in number
daily.
6 And they went through the region of Phrygia and
Galatia, having been forbidden of the Holy Spirit to speak
7 the word **of God to any one** in Asia. And when they were
come over against Mysia, they **wished** to go into Bithynia,
8 and the Spirit **of Jesus** suffered them not. And passing
9 **through** Mysia, they came down to Troas. And **in** a vision

by night there appeared to Paul, **as it were** a certain man of Macedonia, standing **before his face,** beseeching him,
10 and saying, Come over into Macedonia, and help us. When **therefore he had risen up, he related to us the vision,** and we perceived that **the Lord** had called us to preach the Gospel to those who were in Macedonia.
11 **And on the morrow** [therefore] we set sail from Troas, and came with a straight course to Samothrace, and the
12 day following to Neapolis; and from thence to Philippi, which is **the capital** of Macedonia, a city, a colony. And
13 we were in this city tarrying certain days. And on the Sabbath day we went forth without the gate by **the** riverside, where **it seemed likely** that there would be a place of prayer: and we sat down, and spake unto the women
14 which were come together. And a certain woman named Lydia, a seller of purple of the city of Thyatira, one that worshipped God, heard us; whose heart the Lord opened to give heed unto the things which were spoken by Paul.
15 And when she was baptized, and **all** her household, she besought us, saying, If ye have judged me to be faithful to **God,** come into my house, and abide there. And she constrained us.
16 And it came to pass, as we were going to the place of prayer, that a certain maid, having a spirit of divination, met us, which brought her masters much gain **through**
17 **this,** by soothsaying. The same following after Paul and us cried out saying, These men are servants of the Most High God, who proclaim unto you **the good news of**
18 the way of salvation. And this she did for many days. But Paul, **in the Spirit,** turned, and being sore troubled he said, I charge thee in the name of Jesus Christ, that thou come out of her. And **straightway** it came out.
19 But when the masters **of the maiden** saw that they **were deprived of the gain which they had through**

her, they laid hold on Paul and Silas, and dragged them
20 into the market place before the rulers; and when they had
brought them unto the magistrates, they said, These men,
21 being Jews, do exceedingly trouble our city, and set forth
customs which it is not lawful for us to receive or to
22 observe, being Romans. And a **great** multitude rose up
together against them, **crying out.** Then the magistrates
rent their garments off them, and commanded to beat
23 them with rods. And when they had laid many stripes
upon them, they cast them into prison, charging the jailer
24 to keep them safely. And he, having received such a charge,
cast them into the inner prison, and made their feet fast
25 in the stocks. But about midnight Paul and Silas were
praying and singing hymns unto God, and the prisoners
26 were listening to them; and suddenly there was a great
earthquake, so that the foundations of the prison house
were shaken; and immediately all the doors were opened,
27 and every one's bands were loosed. And the jailer being
roused out of sleep, and seeing the prison doors open, drew
his sword, and was about to kill himself, supposing that
28 the prisoners had escaped. But Paul cried with a loud
voice, saying, Do thyself no harm; for we are all here.
29 And he called for lights, and sprang in, and trembling for
30 fear, fell down before **the feet of** Paul and Silas, and led
them out **after securing the rest,** and said, Sirs, what
31 must I do to be saved? And they said, Believe on the
Lord Jesus **Christ,** and thou shalt be saved, thou and
32 thy house. And they spake to him the word of the Lord,
33 with all that were in his house. And he took them the
same hour of the night, and washed their stripes, and
34 was baptized, he and all his, immediately. And he
brought them into his house, and set meat before them,
and rejoiced [greatly] with [all] his house, having believed
in God.

35 But when it was day the magistrates **assembled together into the market place, and recollecting the earthquake that had happened they were afraid; and they** sent the serjeants, saying, Let those men go **whom
36 yesterday thou didst receive.** And the jailer **came in,** and reported the words to Paul, that, The magistrates have sent to let you go: now therefore come forth, and go on
37 your journey [in peace.] But Paul said unto them, **Without fault alleged** they have beaten us publicly, uncondemned, men that are Romans, and have cast us into prison: and do they now cast us out privily? Nay, verily;
38 but let them come themselves and bring us out. And the serjeants reported to the magistrates **themselves** these words **which were spoken for the magistrates;** and
39 when they heard that they were Romans they feared; and they came **with many friends into the prison,** and besought them to go forth, **saying, We did not know about you that ye are just men.** And when they had brought them forth, they besought them, saying, Go forth out of this city, **lest they again assemble against us,
40 crying against you.** And they went out of the prison, and went to Lydia; and when they had seen the brethren, they **reported all the things which the Lord had done for them, and** comforted them and departed.

Chapter XVII

1 Now when they had passed through Amphipolis they **went down** to **Apollonis,** and **thence** to Thessalonica, where
2 was a synagogue of the Jews: and Paul, as his custom was, went in unto them, [and] for three sabbath days discoursed
3 with them from the Scriptures, opening and alleging that it behoved [the] Christ to suffer, and to rise again from the dead, and that this is Christ, Jesus whom, said he, I

XVII 15 TRANSLATED FROM THE CODEX BEZÆ 81

4 proclaim unto you. And some of them were persuaded, and consorted with Paul and Silas, **in the teaching:** and **many** of the devout, **and** of Greeks a great multitude, and women,
5 of the first rank, not a few. But the Jews **who disbelieved assembled** certain vile men of the rabble, [gathering a crowd], and set the city on an uproar, and assaulting the house of Jason, they sought to bring them forth to the
6 people. And when they found them not, they dragged Jason and certain brethren before the rulers of the city, crying out **and saying,** These are they that have turned
7 the world upside down, and have come hither [also]; whom Jason hath received; and these all act contrary to the decrees of Cæsar, saying that there is another king, Jesus.
8 And they troubled the rulers of the city and the multitude.
9 **When they had heard** these things, and when they had taken security from Jason and the rest, they let them go.
10 And the brethren immediately sent away Paul and Silas by night unto Berœa, who when they were come thither
11 went into the synagogue of the Jews. Now these were more noble than those in Thessalonica, in that they received the word with all readiness of mind, examining the Scriptures daily, whether these things were so. **Some** therefore
12 of them believed, **but some did not believe;** and **of the Greeks and of those of honourable estate, both men**
13 **and women, many** believed. But when the Jews from Thessalonica had knowledge that the word of God was proclaimed [of Paul] at Berœa [also], **and that they believed,** they came also thither, and **there did not cease to** stir up
14 and trouble the multitudes. Therefore [immediately] the brethren sent forth Paul to go [as far as] to the sea: but
15 Silas and Timothy abode there still. But they that conducted Paul brought him as far as Athens. **But he passed by* Thessaly for he was forbidden to proclaim the**

* Probably going by sea. But the Latin text has "passed through."

word to them, and receiving a commandment **from Paul** to Silas and Timothy that they should come to him with all speed, they departed.

16 Now while Paul waited for them at Athens, his spirit was provoked within him, as he beheld the city full of idols.
17 So he discoursed in the synagogue with the Jews and the devout persons, and **with those** in the market place every
18 day with them that met with him. And certain also of the Epicurean and Stoic philosophers encountered him. And some said, What would this babbler say? other some, He seemeth to be a setter forth of strange gods, [because he
19 preached Jesus and the Resurrection]. And **after some days** they took hold of him, and brought him unto the Areopagus, **inquiring and** saying May we know what this
20 new teaching is which is spoken by thee? For thou bringest certain strange things to our ears. We would know there-
21 fore what these things mean. Now all the Athenians and the strangers sojourning among them, spent their time in nothing else, but either to tell or to hear some new thing.
22 And Paul stood in the midst of the Areopagus, and said,

Ye men of Athens, in all things I perceive that ye are
23 more than others god-fearing. For as I passed along, and observed the objects of your worship, I found also an altar with the inscription, To an unknown god. What therefore
24 ye worship in ignorance, this set I forth unto you. The God that made the world and all things therein, he, being Lord of heaven and earth, dwelleth not in temples made with
25 hands, neither is he served by men's hands, as though he needed [anything], seeing he himself **gave** to all life and
26 breath and all things. He made of one **blood** every nation of man for to dwell on all the face of the earth; having determined their appointed seasons, **according** to the
27 bound of their habitation; that they should seek **most of all that which is divine,** if haply they might feel after

28 **it, or** find it; though it is not far from each one of us; for in him we live and move, and have our being **day by day.** As certain even of your own [poets] have said, For we are
29 also his offspring. Being then the offspring of God, we ought not to think that the Divine is like unto gold or
30 silver or stone, graven by art and device of man. The times of **this** ignorance therefore. God overlooked; but now he declareth to men that they should all everywhere repent,
31 inasmuch as he hath appointed a day to judge the world in righteousness by the man **Jesus** whom he hath ordained; giving assurance unto all men, in that he hath raised him from the dead.
32 Now when they heard of the resurrection of the dead, some mocked; and others said, We will hear thee concerning
33 this yet again. Thus Paul went out from among them.
34 But certain men clave unto him and believed; among whom also was a **certain** Dionysius **an** Areopagite, [and a woman named Damaris*] of honourable estate, and others with them.

CHAPTER XVIII

1 AND [after these things] he departed from Athens and
2 came to Corinth. And having found a certain Jew named Aquila, a man of Pontus by race, lately come from Italy, and his wife Priscilla, because Claudius had commanded all Jews to depart from Rome: **these had come to dwell**
3 **in Greece; Paul** came unto him, and, because he was of the same trade, abode with them and wrought; [for by
4 their trade they were tentmakers]. And **entering into** the synagogue he discoursed every sabbath, and **introduced the name of the Lord Jesus,** and persuaded not only Jews but also Greeks.

* Possibly a line is omitted in D—and a woman named Damaris—and the word "of honourable estate" applied to her.

5 But **then** Silas and Timothy came from Macedonia, Paul was constrained by the word, testifying to the Jews that
6 the **Lord** Jesus was the Christ. **And after there had been much discourse, and the scriptures had been interpreted,** when they opposed themselves and blasphemed, Paul shook out his raiment, and said unto them, Your blood be upon your own head; I am clean **from you,** [from
7 henceforth] now I go to the Gentiles. And he left **Aquila,** and entered into the house of a certain man named [Titus] Justus, one that worshipped God, whose house joined hard
8 to the synagogue. And Crispus, the ruler of the synagogue, believed on the Lord with all his house; and many of the Corinthians hearing believed, and were baptized **believing in God through the name of our Lord Jesus Christ.**
9 And the Lord said unto Paul by night in a vision, Be
10 not afraid, but speak, and hold not thy peace: for I am with thee, and no man shall set on thee to harm thee,
11 for I have much people in this city. And he dwelt **in Corinth** a year and six months, teaching them the word of God.
12 And when Gallio was proconsul of Achaia, the Jews with one accord rose up, **having talked together amongst themselves** against Paul; **and they laid their hands upon him,** and brought him before the judgment seat,
13 **crying out, and** saying, This man persuadeth men to
14 worship God contrary to the law. But when Paul was about to open his mouth, Gallio said to the Jews, If it were a matter of wrong or of wicked villany, O ye Jews, reason
15 would that I should bear with you: but if ye are **having an** enquiry about words and names and your own law, look to it yourselves. I am not minded to be a judge of these
16 matters. And he drove them from the judgment seat.
17 And **all the Greeks** took hold of Sosthenes, the ruler of the synagogue, and beat him before the judgment seat.

XVIII 28 TRANSLATED FROM THE CODEX BEZÆ 85

Then Gallio pretended not to see him*. [And Gallio cared for none of these things.]
18 And Paul, having tarried after this yet many days took his leave of the brethren, and sailed for Syria, and with him Priscilla and Aquila, having shorn his head in Cen-
19 chreæ: for he had a vow. And **he** came to Ephesus, and **on the next sabbath** he left them there: but he himself entered into the synagogue, and discoursed with the Jews.
20 And when they asked him to abide a longer time, he con-
21 sented not; but taking his leave of them, and saying, I **must by all means keep the coming feast day at Jerusalem,** and return unto you if God will, he set sail from Ephesus.
22 And when he had landed at Cæsarea, he went up and saluted
23 the Church, and went down to Antioch. And having spent some time there he departed, and went through the region of Galatia and Phrygia in order, stablishing all the disciples.
24 Now a certain Jew named **Apollonius,** an Alexandrian by race, a learned man, came to Ephesus; and he was
25 mighty in the scriptures. He had been instructed **in his own country** in the **word** of the Lord; and being fervent in spirit, he spake and taught carefully the things concern-
26 ing Jesus, knowing only the baptism of John. He began to speak boldly in the synagogue. But when Aquila and Priscilla heard him, they took him unto them, and expounded the Way [of God] unto him more carefully.
27 **Now certain Corinthians were sojourning in Ephesus, and having heard him, they exhorted him to cross with them into their own country; and when he consented the Ephesians wrote to the disciples in Corinth that they should receive the man.** And **when he sojourned in Achaia** he helped them much **in the**
28 **churches,** for he powerfully confuted the Jews, **reasoning** publicly, and shewing by the scriptures that Jesus was Christ.

* The translation is from the Latin. The line in Greek is almost entirely erased.

Chapter XIX

1 And **when Paul, according to his private wish, desired to go to Jerusalem, the Spirit told him to return into Asia.** And [while Apollos was at Corinth] he passed through the upper districts and **comes** to Ephesus, and 2 found certain disciples; and he said unto them, Did ye receive the Holy Spirit when ye believed? And they said unto him, Nay, we have not even heard (that) **any receive** 3 **the*** Holy Spirit. And he said, Into what then were ye 4 baptized? And they said, Into John's baptism. And Paul said, John baptized with the baptism of repentance, saying unto the people that they should believe on him which 5 should come after him, that is, on **Christ.** And when they heard this they were baptized into the name of the Lord 6 Jesus **Christ, unto the remission of sins.** And when Paul had laid his hand on them **straightway** the Holy Spirit **fell** upon them: and they spake with tongues, and 7 prophesied. And they were in all about twelve men.

8 And **Paul** entered into the synagogue, and **with great power** spake boldly for the space of three months, discoursing and persuading [as to the things] concerning the 9 kingdom of God. Some **therefore** of them were hardened and unbelieving, and spake evil of the Way before the multitude **of the Gentiles. Then** Paul departed from them, and separated the disciples, discoursing daily in the school of **one** Tyrannus **from the fifth till the tenth hour.** 10 And this continued for [the space of] two years; so that all they that dwelt in Asia heard the words of the Lord, [both] 11 Jews and Greeks. And God wrought special miracles by 12 the hands of Paul; insomuch **even** that unto the sick were carried away from his body handkerchiefs or aprons, and the diseases departed from them, and the evil spirits went

---

* The Bezan text is somewhat confused here.

13 out. But certain [also] of the strolling Jews, exorcists, took upon them to name over them which had the evil spirits the name of the Lord Jesus, saying, I adjure you by Jesus
14 whom Paul preacheth. **Among whom also** [were] the [**seven**] sons of one Sceva, [a Jew] a [chief] priest, [**who**] **wished to do the same thing, being accustomed to exorcise such people. And they came in unto one who was possessed with a devil, and began to call upon the Name saying, We command you, in Jesus whom**
15 **Paul preacheth, to come out. Then the evil spirit** answered and said unto them, Jesus I recognise, and Paul
16 I know: but who are ye? And the man in whom the evil spirit was leaped on them, and mastered both of them, and prevailed against them, so that they fled out of that house
17 naked and wounded. And this became known to all, [both] Jews and Greeks, that dwelt at Ephesus; and fear fell upon them all, and the name of the Lord Jesus was magnified.
18 Many also of them that **were believing**, came confessing
19 and declaring their deeds. And not a few of them that practised curious arts brought also their books together, and burned them in the sight of all; and they counted the prices of them, and found it fifty thousand pieces of
20 silver*. So mightily did it prevail; and the **faith of God** increased and **multiplied.**
21 [Now after these things were ended] then Paul purposed in the Spirit to pass through Macedonia and Achaia, and go to Jerusalem, saying, After I have been there I must
22 also see Rome. And having sent into Macedonia two of them that ministered unto him, Timothy and Erastus, he himself stayed for a **little** while in Asia.
23 And about that time there arose no small stir about the
24 Way. For there was a certain man [named] Demetrius, a silversmith, which made silver shrines of Diana, **who**

* d translates "Two hundred thousand sesterces."

25 brought no little business unto the craftsmen. He gathered together the craftsmen of such things, and said unto them, Fellow craftsmen, ye know that out of this business we have
26 our wealth. And ye hear and see that not alone at Ephesus, but almost throughout all Asia, this Paul, **a somebody,** hath persuaded and turned away much people, saying that
27 they be no gods which are made with hands: and not only is there danger that this our trade come into disrepute; but also that the temple of the great goddess Diana be made of no account, but is about to be deposed [from her magnificence, whom] all Asia and the world worshippeth.
28 And when they heard this, they were filled with wrath, **and they ran into the street,** and cried out saying, Great
29 is Diana of the Ephesians. And the whole city was filled with confusion, and they rushed with one accord into the theatre, having seized Gaius and Aristarchus, men of Mace-
30 donia, Paul's companions in travel. And when Paul was minded to enter in unto the people, the disciples suffered
31 him not. And certain also of the chief officers of Asia, being his friends, sent unto him, and besought him not to adven-
32 ture himself into the theatre. Some therefore cried one thing and some another; for the assembly was in confusion; and the more part knew not wherefore they were come
33 together. And they brought Alexander out of the crowd, the Jews putting him forward. And Alexander beckoned with the hand, and would have made a defence unto the
34 people. But when they perceived that he was a Jew, all with one voice about the space of two hours cried out,
35 Great is Diana of the Ephesians. But the townclerk **beckoned** to the crowd and saith, Ye men of Ephesus, what man is there who knoweth not how that **our** city is temple-keeper of the great Diana, and of the image which
36 fell down from Jupiter? Seeing then that these things cannot be gainsaid, ye ought to be quiet, and to do nothing

37 rash. For ye have brought hither these men, which are neither robbers of temples nor blasphemers of our goddess.
38 If therefore this Demetrius, and the craftsmen that are with him, have **any** matter against **them**, the courts are open, and there are proconsuls; let them accuse one another.
39 But if ye seek anything about other matters, it shall be
40 settled **according to the law of** the assembly. For indeed we are in danger this day to be accused of riot, there being no cause for which we shall be able to give an account of
41 this concourse. And when he had thus spoken he dismissed the assembly.

CHAPTER XX

1 AND after the uproar was ceased, Paul having sent for the disciples, and given them **much** exhortation, took leave
2 of them and departed [for to go] into Macedonia. And when he had gone through those parts, and had given them
3 much exhortation, he came into Greece. And when he had spent three months there, and a plot was laid against him by the Jews he **wished** to sail for Syria. **But the Spirit**
4 **said to him** to return through Macedonia, **therefore when he was about to go out** as far as Asia, Sopater of Berœa, the son of Pyrrhus; and of the Thessalonians Aristarchus and Secundus, and Gaius of Derbe, and Timothy: and **of**
5 **Ephesians Eutychus** and Trophimus. These had gone
6 before and were waiting for **him** at Troas. But we sailed away from Philippi after the days of unleavened bread, and came unto them to Troas in five days; where we
7 tarried seven days. And upon the first day of the week, when we were gathered together to break bread, Paul discoursed with them intending to depart on the morrow, and
8 prolonged his speech until midnight. And there were many lights in the upper chamber, where we were gathered
9 together. And there sat in the window a certain young

man named Eutychus, borne down with deep sleep; and as Paul discoursed yet longer, being borne down by his sleep, he fell down from the third storey and was taken up
10 dead. And Paul went down, and fell on him, and embracing
11 him said, Make ye no ado, for his life is in him. And when he was gone up, and had broken the bread, and had eaten, and had talked with them a long while, even till break of day, so he
12 departed. And **as they were bidding him farewell** they brought the young man alive, and were not a little comforted.
13 But we went* down to the ship, and set sail for Assos, there intending to take in Paul. For so had he appointed,
14 **as** intending himself to go on foot. And, when he met us
15 at Assos, we took him in, and came to Mitylene. And sailing from thence we came the following day over against Chios; and the next day we touched at Samos, **and tarried at Trogyl-**
16 **lium:** and the day after we came to Miletus. For Paul had determined to sail past Ephesus: lest some **detention for him might occur** in Asia, for he was hastening [if it were possible for him] to be in Jerusalem on the day of Pentecost.
17 And from Miletus he sent to Ephesus, and **sent for** the
18 elders of the Church. And when they were come to him, **and were together,** he said unto them, Ye yourselves know, **brethren,** from the first day that I set foot in Asia, **for three years and even more,** after what manner I was
19 with you all the time, serving the Lord, with all lowliness of mind, and with tears, and with trials which befell me
20 by the plots of the Jews: how that I shrank not from declaring unto you all that was profitable, and from teaching
21 from house to house and publicly, testifying both to Jews and to Greeks repentance toward God, and faith **through**
22 our Lord Jesus Christ. And now, behold, I go bound in the spirit unto Jerusalem, not knowing the things which
23 shall befall me there, save that the Holy Spirit testifieth

* *a* reads "we, going before to the ship, set sail."

unto me in every city saying that bonds and afflictions
24 abide me in Jerusalem. But I take account of none of these
things, nor hold my life as dear unto myself, that I may
accomplish my course and the ministry **of the word** which
I received from the Lord Jesus to testify **to Jews and**
25 **Greeks** the gospel of the grace of God. And now, behold,
I know, that ye all among whom I went about preaching
26 the kingdom **of Jesus** shall see my face no more. Therefore
[I testify unto you that] **until** this day I am pure from the
27 blood of all men. For I shrank not from declaring unto you
28 the whole counsel of God. Take heed unto yourselves and
to all the flock, in the which the Holy Spirit hath made you
bishops, to feed the Church of **the Lord** which he purchased
29 for himself with his own blood. I know that after my
departing grievous wolves shall enter in among you, not
30 sparing the flock; and from among your own selves shall
men arise, speaking perverse things, to draw away the
31 disciples after them. Wherefore watch ye, remembering
that by the space of three years I ceased not to admonish
32 every one night and day with tears. And now I commend
you to God, and to the word of his grace, which is able to
build you up, and to give you inheritance among [all] them
33 that are sanctified. I coveted **of you all** no man's silver,
34 or gold, or apparel. Ye yourselves know that **my** hands
ministered unto my necessities, and to [all] them that were
35 with me. In all things I gave you an example, that so
labouring ye ought to help the weak, [and] to remember
the words of the Lord Jesus how that he himself said,
It is more blessed to give than to receive.
36 And when he had thus spoken, he kneeled down, and
37 prayed with them all. And they all wept sore, and fell on
38 Paul's neck, and kissed him; sorrowing most of all for the
word which he spake, Ye shall see my face no more. And
they brought him on his way unto the ship.

Chapter XXI

1 AND when [it came to pass that] we had set sail and were parted from them, we came with a straight course unto Cos, and the next day unto Rhodes, and from thence unto Patara
2 **and Myra;** and having found a ship crossing unto Phœnice.

> One leaf is missing here, containing xx. 31 to xxi. 2 in Latin, and xxi. 2–10 in Greek.

Chapter XXI. 10

10
11 ...prophet named Agabus. And coming **up** to us, and taking Paul's girdle, he bound his own feet and hands, and said, Thus saith the Holy Spirit, so shall the Jews at Jerusalem bind the man that owneth this girdle, and shall
12 deliver him into the hands of the Gentiles. And when we heard these things, both we and they of that place besought
13 **Paul** not **himself** to go up to Jerusalem. But Paul said to us, What do ye, weeping and **disturbing** my heart; for I **desire** not to be bound only but am ready also to die at
14 Jerusalem for the name of the Lord Jesus **Christ.** And when he would not be persuaded, we ceased, saying **to one another,** The will of **God** be done.
15 And after **certain** days* we **bade them farewell,** and
16 we go up to Jerusalem **from Cæsarea;** and with us **those**
17 **who led us to** him with whom we should lodge. And **when they came to a certain village, we stayed with** Nason†, a certain Cyprian, an old disciple; and **going forth thence** we came to Jerusalem. And the brethren received us gladly.
18 And the day following Paul went in with us unto James,
19 ‡and the elders were assembled **with him.** And when he

* In this text it is plain that from Cæsarea to Jerusalem is a two days' journey: and they travelled with him to introduce him to Mnason who was to entertain him for the first night. The *a* text for "bade them farewell" reads "took up our baggage."
† Verses 15–18 are wanting in the Greek text.
‡ The Greek text begins again here.

had saluted them he rehearsed one by one the things which
20 God had wrought among the Gentiles by his ministry. And
when they heard it they glorified **the Lord,** saying, Thou
seest, brother, how many myriads there are **in Judæa** of
them which have believed, and they are all zealous for the
21 law; and they have been informed concerning thee, that
thou teachest [all] the Jews which are among the Gentiles
to forsake Moses, telling them not to circumcise their
22 children, neither to walk after their customs. What is it
therefore? **The multitude must needs come together,**
23 **for** they will [certainly] hear that thou art come. Do therefore this that we say to thee. We have four men which have
24 a vow on them; these take, and purify thyself with them,
and be at charges for them, that they may shave their
heads; and all may know that there is no truth in the things
whereof they have been informed concerning thee; but that
25 thou thyself also walkest orderly, keeping the law. But as
touching the Gentiles which have believed, **they have
nothing to say against thee, for** we sent giving judgment, **that they should observe nothing of that sort,**
except to **guard** themselves from idol sacrifices, and from
blood, [and from what is strangled], and from fornication.
26 Then Paul took the men, and the next day purifying himself with them he went into the temple, declaring the
fulfilment of the days of purification until the offering was
made for every one of them.

27 And when the seven days were [almost] completed, the
Jews **who had come** from Asia, when they saw him in
the temple, stirred up all the multitudes, and laid hands
28 upon him, crying out, Men of Israel, help: This is the man
that teacheth all men everywhere against the people, and
the law, and this place; and moreover he brought Greeks
29 into the temple, and hath defiled this holy place. For they
had before seen with him in the city Trophimus the

Ephesian, whom they supposed that Paul had brought into
30 the temple. And all the city was moved, and the people ran
together: and they laid hold on Paul, and dragged him out
of the temple: and straightway, the doors were shut. And
31 as they were seeking to kill him, tidings came up to the
chief captain of the band, that all Jerusalem was in con-
32 fusion. And forthwith he took soldiers and centurions and
ran down upon them: and they, when they saw the chief
33 captain and the soldiers, left beating of Paul. Then the
chief captain came near, and laid hold on him, and commanded him to be bound with two chains, and enquired
34 who he was and what he had done. And some shouted one
thing, and some another, among the crowd; and when he
could not know the certainty for the uproar, he commanded
35 him to be brought into the castle. And when he came upon
the stairs, so it was, that he was borne of the soldiers for
the violence of the people: for the multitude [of the people]
36 followed after, crying out, Away with him.

37 And as he was about to be brought into the castle, he
answered and said to the chief captain, May I speak unto
38 thee? And he said, Dost thou know Greek? Art thou not
[then] the Egyptian, which before these days stirred up to
sedition, and led out into the wilderness, the four thousand
39 men of the Assassins? But Paul said, I am a Jew, **born in**
Tarsus of Cilicia, [a citizen of no mean city], and I beseech
40 thee give me leave to speak unto the people. And when
the chief Captain had given him leave, Paul, standing on
the stairs, beckoned with the hand unto the people: and
when there was made a great silence, he spake unto them
in the Hebrew language, saying:

Chapter XXII

1 Men, Brethren and fathers, hear ye my defence which I
2 make now unto you. And when they heard that he spake

[unto them] in the Hebrew language, they were the more
3 quiet; and he saith, I am a Jew, born in Tarsus of Cilicia, but brought up in this city at the feet of Gamaliel, instructed according to the strict manner of the law of our fathers,
4 zealous for God, even as ye all are this day. And I persecuted this Way unto death, binding and delivering into
5 prison both men and women. As also the high priest **will** bear witness to me, and all the estate of the elders, from whom I received letters from the brethren. I was journeying to Damascus, to bring them also that were there unto Jerusalem in bonds, that they might be
6 punished. And [it came to pass that as I made my journey], as I drew nigh unto Damascus, about noon, suddenly
7 there shone from heaven a great light round about me, and I fell unto the ground, and heard a voice saying unto me,
8 Saul, Saul, why persecutest thou me? And I answered, Who art thou, Lord? And he said unto me, I am Jesus
9 **of Nazareth** whom thou persecutest. And they that were with me saw indeed the light, **and were frightened;** but
10 they heard not the voice of him that spake with me. And I said, What shall I do, Lord. And **he** said unto me, Arise, and go into Damascus, and there it shall be told thee of
11 all things* which thou oughtest to do. But **when I rose up** I did not see for the glory of that light, and being led by the hand of them that were with me I came into
12 Damascus. And one Ananias, a devout man according to
13 the law, and by the witness of all the Jews, came unto me and [standing by me] said unto me, **Saul,** Brother Saul, receive thy sight; and in that very hour I received sight.
14 And he said **unto me,** The God of our fathers hath appointed thee to know his will, and to see the Righteous one, and to
15 hear a voice from his mouth; for thou shalt be a witness for him unto all men of what thou hast seen and heard.

* From this verse to v. 20 the Greek text is wanting. The Latin remains.

16 And now, why tarriest thou? Arise, be baptized, and wash
17 away thy sins, calling on his name. And it came to pass
that when I had returned to Jerusalem and while I prayed
18 in the temple, I fell into a trance, and saw him saying unto
me, Make haste and get thee quickly out of Jerusalem
because they will not receive **my** testimony [from thee.]
19 And I said, Lord, they themselves know that I imprisoned
and beat in every synagogue them that believed on thee:
20 and when the blood of Stephen the witness was shed, I
[also] was standing by, and consenting*, and keeping the
21 garments of them that slew him. And he said unto me,
Depart, for I send thee forth far hence unto the Gentiles.
22 And they gave him audience unto this word: and they
lifted up their voice and said, Away with such a fellow
23 from the earth, for it is not fit that he should live. And as
they cried out, and threw off their garments, and cast dust
24 into the air, the chief captain commanded him to be
brought into the castle, bidding that he should be examined
by scourging, that he might know for what cause they so
25 shouted against him. And when they had tied him up
with the thongs, he said unto the centurion that stood by,
Is it lawful for you to scourge a man that is a Roman and
26 uncondemned. And when the centurion heard this, **that
he called himself a Roman** he went to the chief captain
and told him, **See** what thou art about to do. This man is
27 a Roman. Then the chief captain came **and asked him,**
28 Tell me, art thou a Roman? and he said, I am. And the
chief captain answered, **I know** with how great a sum I
obtained this citizenship. And Paul said, But I am [a
29 Roman] born. Then they departed from him...

All the rest of the Codex Bezæ is wanting.

* Here the Greek is preserved, and the Latin is wanting.

www.ingramcontent.com/pod-product-compliance
Lightning Source LLC
Chambersburg PA
CBHW070302100426
42743CB00011B/2311